Raccoons in Our Bathroom

Kathryn C. Bode

PAGE PUBLISHING, INC.
Conneaut Lake, PA

First originally published by Page Publishing 2020

ISBN 978-1-64584-356-6 (pbk)
ISBN 978-1-64584-357-3 (digital)

Printed in the United States of America

Dedication

To my parents, for teaching me respect and love of all living things; to Gordon, my husband and lifelong partner, for his love and help with my wild life; to my two wonderful daughters, Jeaneil and Robin, and now also my granddaughter, Angeline, for being here when I need them the most; to my sister, Jeanine, who helped convince other relatives that I was not crazy; to Susie, who guided me through my first of over twenty summers raising orphaned wildlife and became a trusted friend in the process; to Mary—, who volunteered to proofread these pages and write the special foreword I'll try to live up to; and dear Mona, who gave me the opportunity to write in her raccoon newsletter about my adventures with raccoons.

You all have a special place in my heart!

Kathryn Bode

Contents

Preface

In the beginning, God created the heaven and earth. He proceeded from there to divide the light from the darkness, the land from the heavens, and gathered the waters into what he called seas. Next, he covered the land with grasses, trees, and all growing things. With great joy, he brought forth all living creatures to roam the earth and fill the seas, and he was pleased.

Then God said, "Let us make man in our image." Male and female created he them.

As an eon or more passed, the animals and their offspring fell into distress as mankind encroached upon their habitat. Saddened by the situation, God felt the need to bring forth guardians, caregivers, and protectors of his wildlife. For the animals, such persons become special angels, and author Kathryn Bode numbers among them.

Kathryn is a person who has truly dedicated herself to the care and preservation of wildlife. Always aware of animals in need, she found her true calling one summer morning in 1988 when a desperate, homeless baby raccoon looked up into her eyes and called her "mom."

Raccoons in Our Bathroom is more than a story about raccoon rescue; it is the perfect lesson to teach any skeptic that animals think, feel, fear, worry, and love—just like you and me. Kathryn boldly invites us into her life, her home, and her heart, and what a delightfully enriching adventure it is. She skillfully describes the insecurities and unbelievable humorous antics of baby coons that all too soon would be hungering for their freedom.

For anyone who has the capacity to share love with an animal and believes that in God's hands is the soul of every living thing (scripture), this book is a must-read. Of all his children, I suspect that God is supremely pleased and eternally grateful for that one dear soul—Kathryn Bode. Foster mom, healer, advocate, educator, and now one that many animals have lovingly called mom.

Mary Garwood
Author, *Pawprints Upon My Heart*

TAIL ONE

Ricky Raccoon

Meeting a Bigmouth

T his is the story of the first summer I raised orphaned raccoons and how it changed my life. My husband, Gordon, and I live in the small village of Cherry Valley, Illinois. It is just outside Rockford and near the Wisconsin border. My parents have a permanent home on Lake Wisconsin, a few miles north of Madison.

My assorted family members go up to visit them as often as possible, so on the Memorial Day weekend of 1988, I was looking forward to being with everyone and enjoying some peace and quiet. Little did l know that this was wishful thinking.

I awoke that first morning to my five-year-old niece, Kristin, banging on my bedroom door. She was yelling excitedly for me to come and see what she had found. I am not a morning person but managed to get moving and ten minutes later, I was following her outside.

It was a beautiful day though it had really stormed the night before. I wondered if it would get warm enough to take a first swim of the summer season. All thought of swimming (or doing anything else) flew right out of my mind, however. I heard a strange, earsplitting noise that sounded like a very young, hungry human baby.

Staggering down the sidewalk was the saddest, scruffiest ball of fur I had ever seen. It seemed to be all mouth. I couldn't believe something that small could be putting up such a commotion.

"What is *it?*" Kristin asked.

As we watched it hone in on our voices, it instantly changed direction and dashed toward us. I told her it might be a raccoon, reserving judgement until I could get a better look. My brain went into high gear as I tried to remember something—anything—about raccoons.

I remembered as children, my sister, brother, and I had brought home many sick, injured, or unwanted animals—much to Mom's dismay. Our father, however, took the prize for rescuing the various nonhuman guests. Rags, our dog at the time, became quite upset when someone came into the house, carrying a box. We had never come across an orphaned raccoon during our childhood so I guess it was only a matter of time, and my time had just run out.

The day Kristin and I hovered over the fuzzy kid, we finally decided it was a raccoon.

Yes, that's what it was all right. A crowd of curious family members gathered around to watch the coon demanding attention. Someone mentioned rabies, and perhaps we should just leave it alone, but try ignoring a hungry, wild raccoon baby. It's noise could probably have been heard all the way to Lodi, Wisconsin, about fifteen miles away.

I knew that wildlife rabies was not common in the Midwest and decided to pick up the baby. Its tune changed from a desperate alarm to a questioning whistle that I would come to know very well. The first thing I discovered was that "it" was a he and the first thing he discovered was that I looked like a "mom." His eyes couldn't focus very well, but he thought my finger might be something to eat. He began sucking my thumb by curling his tongue around it, and thank goodness, he had no teeth to speak of. When no milk appeared, he began to suck harder, and I do mean harder.

Dad brought out a cardboard box and Mom put some old towels in it. Next, we all began a treasure hunt for something to put warm milk in. The only thing available was an old plastic hair-dye bottle. I boiled it and then filled it with milk.

I sat at the picnic table with the little squirming fur ball, his sharp toenails wrapped around my hand, and began an attempt to feed him. At first, he looked at me very suspiciously and did his pathetic little whistle. Finally hunger overcame his fear and he chowed down.

Kristin had been watching intently and suddenly burst out with, "Hey, he doesn't have a name." So, we rattled off just about every boy's name we had ever heard of that might be a good one for an animal. Kristin finally came up with Ricky, and it seemed to suit him.

Ricky caught on to getting the milk from that improvised bottle pretty quickly and, in the middle of being named, christened himself by unscrewing the bottle lid. The milk splashed all over both of us. Most of his first meal in captivity was sucked off from his fur, my hand, and my clothes. After an hour of eating and being played with, Ricky curled up in his box and slept. Kristin gave him a stuffed animal to keep him company. I put a towel over the box and placed it on the picnic table just in case any loose dogs came by while we were busy elsewhere.

I went in to get myself a very late breakfast and though I didn't really forget about the raccoon, I still jumped when four hours later, I heard a "Whaaaah! Whaaaah!" When I looked in the box, his little chin was quivering, and he looked so helpless and pathetic. Feeding and amusing him and he amusing the rest of us continued for the rest of the long Memorial Day weekend.

But as time went by, I began to think seriously about what would happen to Ricky when we all went home on Monday and Tuesday. With all the things Mom and Dad had going on in their lives, they really didn't have the time for a raccoon baby. I didn't work outside the home, but what did I really know about raising a raccoon? Well, I had already raised two daughters so…?

My sister Jeanine, and my niece Kristin, and I went for one of our many walks. We found a tree that had fallen during the storm the night before. There were signs that Ricky's family had lived there and left him accidentally behind when they got away from their destroyed home. We discussed the possibility that the mother raccoon had relocated the family and was worried and missing Ricky. On Saturday night, we put his box on the upper deck where his mom would come and get him if he called to her.

Well, he called all right! This time I think they could hear him in Madison about half an hour away. Because of all his racket, we got very little sleep. I am sure the people on vacation in the surrounding cottages were thrilled with the Wrasse clan. After trying to return Ricky to his mom for two nights in a row, I decided to call the nearest DNR (Department of Natural Resources). I wanted some advice and hopefully, some help.

The person I spoke to on the phone was nice enough, but he said it was not possible for anyone there to take the time to raise a baby coon. Now, what was I to do? By Monday, I had decided that this little fellow could not survive in the wild on his own. He had no teeth, was still nursing, and Ricky was not old enough to be independent of outside help. We had pretty much decided I could be his mom temporarily, and why not be his foster mother until he got older? Why not indeed!

Before I made a final decision, I got an umbrella and took the coon kid several properties away. I put him down in the drizzling rain. Maybe he could find his mother on his own, I hoped. But the rain probably had washed away any footprint or smell that could have helped him, so Ricky wandered and cried but didn't really go anywhere. After an hour or so, the strategy was getting old for me, not to mention he was cold and wet. My mom called from her dry and cozy upper deck. "What's he doing?"

When I answered back, "Not much," the foster kid heard my voice and came scampering back. He quickly found me, climbed up my pant leg, and was in my arms so fast I didn't know what hit me. I had a pretty good idea though.

Dad laughed and said, "Well he's yours now." That was the understatement of the year!

"I guess it's back to the good old cardboard box," I muttered to Rick.

That night, I was pretty tired and since I had a two-hour drive home to Cherry Valley on Tuesday afternoon, I asked my dad to please feed Ricky in the early morning for me. My father had toyed with the idea of raising the raccoon himself and releasing him back on their property. But he and Mom liked to take spur-of-the-moment trips which was the reason why they didn't have any pets. Mom and Dad fostered human teenagers for years, but when Dad retired, they wanted some excitement in their lives. I don't think raccoons fit into that plan. Besides, it's bad enough to take a dog or cat with you on a trip, but a baby raccoon? I don't think so!

Anyway, Dad got up with Rick or probably Rick got Dad up early. When I came out later in the morning, I noticed Dad lying out on the upper deck. As I got closer, I could see he was on his stomach with a very contented-looking furry baby lying across the back of his neck. I took a photo of it, and as you may have guessed, they were both fast asleep. It was a special scene that I will always remember because it was the last time my dad would ever help me with an animal. I am sure he's up in heaven smirking down as he watches me deal with all the furry foster kids I have had, starting with "Ricky Raccoon."

A Crash Course in Coons

On Tuesday, Ricky, his box, and I went home to Cherry Valley in my minivan. He was almost too quiet in the car. He was probably trying to figure out where he was going and what was going to happen to him next. Luckily, we had no adventures on the way home. I found out later that transporting a live wild animal across state lines is against the law. It is, however, alright to transport dead ones. Go figure!

I had forewarned my husband, Gordon, by telephone that we would be having an unusual houseguest. We had taken in animals before but in most cases, not too successfully. Maybe this time we would do better, maybe not. But whatever happened, Gordon was looking forward to meeting the tiny guy. Little did he know how I planned to recruit him for either the late-night feedings or the early-morning ones. Both would be even better. After all, he worked the late shift at his "real" job.

Our two dogs greeted me at the door as usual and were not even suspicious of the box I was holding. Their ears really perked up though when they heard that questioning whistle. They knew it was not coming from me. Abby, at ten, was our resident mothering mutt, being part bearded collie and part Heinz 57. Toto, our three-year-old terrier mix, was a sad, retarded little thing who spent most of her time sleeping on the rug in the bathroom. She hardly knew the baby raccoon was in the house until weeks later when we put Ricky in the bathroom and Toto had to give up her space.

Since I knew next to nothing about raccoons, I let my fingers do the walking. By telephone, I tried to get some advice from our veterinarian, the Illinois Conservation Department, and assorted animal-lover groups. Finally, I was given the name of a licensed wildlife animal rehabilitator who lived less than two miles from us right in Cherry Valley.

After several conversations with Susie, she came over to take a look at our resident bigmouth. She told me to stop giving him cow's milk as most wildlife babies' stomachs and intestines cannot tolerate it as a steady diet. Susie showed me how to mix a special powered-milk substitute with warm water to use instead. She had many other helpful hints to pass along as well.

Baby raccoons have a very strong sucking reflex as I had found out earlier. What I didn't know was that they would not stop eating when they were full. They can get sick or worse if the amount they eat is not regulated. So much to learn! I realized this could get complicated.

Suzie loaned me some books about coons and made sure I read the part about diseases. Raccoons usually have roundworms and must be medicated for that. Distemper is epidemic in our area though not dangerous to humans. Currently, there are no documented cases of rabies in Illinois raccoons. If there had been, we would not be able to have them in our possession. Raising orphaned wildlife is not as much fun or as easy as it sounds. Veterinarians are too busy in most cases to help. But I have been lucky enough to find two vets who help me.

Susie was up to her ears in raccoons that summer I found Ricky. She was also worried that a couple of her animals were possibly sick with distemper, and she did not want to give it to him. I had planned to turn Ricky over to her even though my heart was not in it. I wanted the raccoon to have the best chance to survive and be healthy enough to be released back to the wild when he was older.

I guess Susie thought I acted like a raccoon mother as she actually asked me if I would like to raise him with her help. Little did she know how many phone calls a week she was going to get from me.

She never seemed to lose patience with me. I know that without her encouragement, I could not have made it through that summer.

That first day, Susie also explained that it was against the law to keep any wild animal as a pet. Even rehabbers must release the critters back to the wild as soon as feasible. She had a conservation permit to keep wildlife. I could work under her and it would be legal. This law has since changed. Unless you have your own permit, you cannot keep a wild animal, period. And unless one has a federal permit, you can't even handle birds or endangered species. If a person does not have a permit and keeps a wild animal as a pet, there is a five-hundred-dollar fine if they get caught. The animal is usually destroyed too.

Susie and I immediately became fast friends. From her, I learned that Ricky was about six weeks old. This is a bad age for coons, sort of like the "terrible twos" in human children. They wander away from their mom and are easily sidetracked, hence they "get lost." Their howling soon gets their mom's attention, and she rescues them from whatever mess they've gotten themselves into. That is, unless something permanent has happened to her. Raccoon mothers take their responsibilities quite seriously and teach their children all sorts of survival techniques. Now, it was up to me to learn what to do.

Ricky's teeth, or lack of them, were the biggest clue to his age. The texture of his fur was another. As coons get older, the fur changes from a sort of wispy down to a thick and course bristle with guard hairs. There is a definite, color-change line also as they mature.

Reading about raccoons led me to have a healthy respect for their intelligence and ability to survive under almost any condition. This was a very interesting animal that I was about to foster for the summer. I just hope he thought I was interesting too. He certainly didn't seem to mind being here.

Gordon took an active part in handling Ricky and many mornings, the kid would end up on the floor with him, sleeping on his neck after he had been fed. It gave me a chance to wake up and get my act together. Gordon also took many of the late-night feedings willingly.

Ricky Settles in and Unsettles Us

I f our new child thought I looked like a raccoon mother, he was really impressed with his new dad. Gordon had red hair that was a tad longer than normal and a bushy red-and-gray beard. So now, we had a "son of fur-face." Ricky loved to feel Gordon's beard, but sometimes those nasty, razor-sharp claws would unintentionally scratch him. Ouch!

All the rehabbers who met Ricky said he was the most beautiful raccoon they had ever seen. Don't think he didn't know it. Besides his unusual beauty, I learned that the name Ricky was a very common one for a raccoon, and we all knew this was no ordinary raccoon. So, this led me to change his name to Pooh Bear as that was exactly what he reminded me of. Eventually, just yelling "Pooh" would get his instant attention.

Susie mentioned, in one of our many telephone conversations, that my coon really should have another raccoon to be raised with. Now, that was something to look forward to—two of them. But the real reason Pooh needed a friend was that he had to find out he was a raccoon baby and not a human one. And the sooner, the better for all concerned too.

Pooh, on instinct, would follow Mom (me) around the house as fast as his little legs would carry him. If I walked too fast, I was reminded in no uncertain terms to slow down. He could be very loud about it too. I learned what all the different sounds he made meant, and I got pretty good at mimicking them. I was at least good enough to fool my little scamp and hopefully keep us both out of trouble. I have already mentioned the questioning whistle and of course, the "*Whaa whaa*, I am hungry right now" tone, but his vocabulary got more complicated as he got older. He also had a loud growl whenever he felt threatened. That rumble was ferocious and funny at the same time coming from such a little guy. Last, but not least, in the wild, when the coon mom stomps her foot and hisses at the same time, it means that "baby" had better shape up right now. I only used this tactic when he was truly in danger, and he always obeyed.

Baby coons climb on and wrestle with their natural mothers, so I learned the hard way not to wear favorite blouses or snaggy slacks. And long pants are a much better choice than wearing shorts. Pooh liked to climb up my legs and get a better look at what I was doing. He hoped to maybe lend a helping paw. Pooh seemed to have the brains of a very smart dog and the agility of a cat; not a good combination, I would say.

I learned to never step backward without looking to see where the little mischief maker was. If I stepped on him, I heard about it! The dogs would run whenever they heard that noise and as far away as possible. I wore some favorite old white canvas shoes a lot that summer, and Pooh accepted them as his mom's normal feet. One day, I had different shoes on, and I could not figure out why he was acting so confused. When he realized it was me, in different feet, he perked right up.

Our older dog, Abby, would watch intently while I fed the bottomless pit every four to five hours. She had to sniff him every time I was ready to put him in his box. Upon being asked where her baby was, Abby would run to the box, stick her head in, assure me that Pooh was all right, and then wag her tail. When Pooh got older, he wasn't quite as willing to go into his box. If I really needed to leave him howling in the box, Abby made a great coon sitter. She would watch to make sure he didn't climb out. Judging by the look on her face, Abby didn't appreciate dealing with the noise though. When Pooh did get out of the box, he would crawl onto Abby and look for lunch. After trying for several days in a row, Pooh finally gave up that idea and would just end up playing with her fur. Abby would wince and occasionally curl her lip half-heartedly, but she always came back for more.

I hated letting Pooh get used to the dogs because who knows what situation he would come across when he was finally released? Would he know a friendly dog from a mean one?

After eating, it was "nap time," and Pooh began to procrastinate as much as possible. It wasn't long before the little cardboard box seemed to shrink. Suddenly, one day, a not so little coon just climbed right out without doggy help, and that was that! Now, I wondered, *Where do we put him for his shorter and shorter coon naps?*

We began to shut him in the bathroom at night. It was like trying to put a two-year old human child to bed. One big problem was that raccoons are night creatures, and most of us people are not. We compromised by tucking him in at 3:00 AM and allowing him to sleep later in the morning. My kind of kid!

Many pictures were taken of Pooh Bear. After the first few bouts with a camera's flash, he began to cover his eyes every time he saw the camera. He knew his name and was litter box-trained almost at once. He also minded fairly well (when he was in the mood). But if it sounds like raccoons make good pets, forget it! Besides the mischief coons make, they are wild animals and become more independent as they get older. They growl, hiss, and begin to have a wild odor as they become teenagers. They can also bite if they don't get their way or feel threatened. In other words, they are no longer cutesy or fun.

Of course, Pooh had a way to go before this happened to him, and we were going to enjoy each other as long as we could. At least we would be pals until a raccoon friend could be found for him. As I said earlier, Pooh was litter trained. Very young mammals must be stimulated by their mothers to relieve themselves. I found that using tissue and doing this over a litter box helped him get the idea to "go" in there. Later, I exchanged the litter for torn-up newspapers because half the cat litter would end up all over the place. If given a choice, a wild animal will not soil the area where they sleep, and intelligent raccoons catch on quickly.

A Gardener with Four Green Thumbs

I tried to give Pooh as normal a life for his kind as possible. Raccoons aren't usually found chasing a vacuum cleaner around or sleeping in a bathroom. For many reasons, I took Pooh outside as often as possible. In decent weather, I had to make the time to become a teacher. We have two acres with lots of grass, trees, and places to explore, including a swimming pool. There were also plenty of gardening chores to be done, and I was pretty much behind schedule out in the yard that spring. (I wonder why?)

I still don't remember hiring my helper for the spring of 1988, however. I had a hard time letting Pooh just run around the yard. Other rehabbers let their animals, even squirrels, run loose with good results. I was still nervous the first few times I took him out into the great outdoors. Pooh wanted to stay on my shoulder as I walked around doing small yard chores those first few days. Eventually, his curious nature finally won out over fear. It also helped when he got reacquainted with all the natural sounds such as birds chirping, dogs barking, traffic on the bypass, and breezes blowing in his face.

One day, I was planting tulip bulbs right behind the house. I was trying to place them in a pleasing arrangement. Pooh was watching every move I made. Dig a little hole, put the roundish thing in it, and cover it up—this looked easy. I could see him practicing his hole-digging skills out of the corner of my eye as I made a nice, straight row. After about half an hour, I got up to stretch my legs, and I took a better look to see what my little worker was doing.

There were the bulbs I had just planted. Yes, there they were—all of them—in a perfectly neat row on top of the dirt, and Pooh was sitting there looking so pleased with himself.

I also had lots of help cleaning up some broken glass in the back of our property. Pooh never cut himself as he carefully placed each piece in the bucket, just like Mom. I was pretty leery about letting him examine the possibly sharp pieces, but I couldn't keep him away from the pretty-colored "sparklys."

Sometimes, I would be so involved in an outside project that I would forget my coon was just a baby. What always happens when a baby gets tired? You guessed it: they get crabby. You haven't lived until you have had an overly tired raccoon on your hands. But Mommy came prepared with a bottle of formula in her pocket so she wouldn't have to trek all the way back to the house. Hey, I raised two human children, and I learned a few tricks of the trade. At this point in the story, Pooh and I took a break for a sort of picnic lunch. All the fresh air had made him sleepy and me, too, by the way. Pooh would crawl up on my shoulder and sleep deeply as only the exhausted young can. I learned to pull weeds and do assorted other chores with him snoring across my neck. I even became good at standing up, walking, and making it to the house without waking him up. Then, when I would try to put him in his box, or in the bathroom, coon baby would open his eyes and seemed to say, "I don't think so. Short naps are great."

On another occasion, I had help pulling weeds in an old truck tire we had turned into a flower box. The phone rang, and I went to answer it on the cordless telephone I had left on the picnic table. As I talked, I kept an eye on my enthusiastic green-thumbed kid. I was amazed upon my return to the planter. Pooh had pulled all the weeds and left the flowers intact and all for less-than-minimum wage. I wondered if he did windows. Most of the ones on the first floor of our house had nose and paw prints all over the lower half of them.

Our younger daughter, Robin, came out to help me rake leaves, but we really didn't get much accomplished. We were too busy being entertained by our resident ham. Pooh loved to climb in Robin's natural long blond hair and wondered why she didn't wear glasses like Mom.

Teaching a Tyrant

Teaching Pooh how to climb trees wasn't too difficult for me. I fed him at the base of the tree, and he would look way up, and then climb me instead. Once I convinced him to go up the tree, he caught on pretty quickly. Coming down was another matter. More than once, I had to haul out the long ladder and go after a whimpering little one. When I would reach for him, he would run down my arm and onto my head where he would hang on for dear life. After weeks of practice, he would zip twenty feet up a tree so tall I couldn't believe it. He was like a fuzzy blur. Sometimes he didn't feel like coming back down when I wanted him to though. I can't count the times I was late going somewhere because I was trying to lure that raccoon out of a tree. He got pretty suspicious of my sweet-talking, and I had to resort to bribery. Marshmallows always seemed to do the trick.

Things I took for granted were learning experiences for a young and an inexperienced raccoon. His hands would never stop feeling around for new things to check out, though the eyes never left my face. Occasionally, he would put something in his mouth to see if it was edible. I began to sprinkle cheerios and other goodies around in the grass to help him learn to forage for natural food.

I have never met an animal so into himself as Pooh and probably never will again. A mirror was at first something shiny and smooth to examine. I couldn't decide for certain what went on in his little mind when he saw his paws or my face in the mirror. Did he realize who it was? He looked behind it many times though, as if looking for the rest of whoever it was he saw there.

When Pooh was small, it didn't take much to keep him happy. Just being fed, well rested, and with me satisfied him for the first couple of weeks. The naps and attention span got shorter every day, right along with my patience. Before I knew it, I was spending half my life with the baby, partly just watching him explore. It was kind of sad to think that his first experiences in the world were not with his real family in the great outdoors where he belonged. I wondered, Did his natural mother miss him, if she was still alive? Would he survive when he was finally freed and truly on his own? Would he remember me? Would he be so imprinted on me that he wouldn't be able to survive being separated from me?

I went to garage sales and got him all sorts of educational toys. Pooh's favorite was a big plastic ball with different shaped holes in it. I showed him how the different shaped pieces went in the appropriate holes. Pooh wanted his turn to try. Left to his own devices, he got about half of them right. When pieces wouldn't fit into the holes he wanted them to, he rejected them by flinging the pieces halfway across the floor. Then he would lie down, kicking and screaming like any two-year-old. When his temper tantrums were over, he would go back to exploring his artificial world under the watchful eyes of "foster Mom."

Pooh trashed my house plants, harassed the two dogs, rearranged things on the lower shelves, and sat mesmerized by the television. Our cockatiel, Rascal, was not impressed with Pooh's newfound climbing abilities, however. He climbed up the drapes after her just once and came down a lot faster than he went up. Pooh also taught himself to pull open kitchen cupboards, but there were only pots and pans in there to rattle around. This was very distracting to me, especially when I was on the phone, then he did acrobatic tricks with the phone cord.

Water, Water...Everywhere

I n my quest to learn as much as I could about raccoons, it was
obvious that every book mentioned their love of water. Raccoons
fish streams, rivers, and anywhere else that they might find crayfish—their favorite food. My Pooh's first experience with water was a
learning experience for me as well.

I took him out onto our open front porch along with a twelve-
by-nine cake pan half full of water. He put on his great I'm-not-
interested act and felt all along the porch floor with his front paws.
As he got closer and closer to the pan, he continued to keep his
eyes fastened on my face trying to read my expression like always,
seeming able to sense my many moods and act accordingly. On this
sunny spring day, the looks passed between us must have conveyed
a positive message that I wouldn't give him anything dangerous. He
felt near the edge of the pan but had not actually touched the strange
silver object that he really wanted to check out quite desperately. A
breeze rippled the water, and he scuttled away with his eyes popping
out of his head, only to edge closer all over again. After many cau-
tious investigations from all angles, Pooh became braver. Curiosity
in a coon is perhaps their strongest personality trait. Luckily, caution
is just about as strong. *Pat, pat, pat* went the front paws as he crept
closer, pretending to be more interested in an acorn he had just stum-
bled over. Finally, after half an hour, he actually touched the pan, and
it didn't attack him. This felt safe, but what's the sloshy goop inside?
Is it alive or what?

Earlier that day, Pooh had shredded an earthworm and had gummed to death several June bugs the day before. This was something new to be dealt with. So much to learn about. I tried to understand what went through his little brain when he finally stuck his paw in the water. It was love at first feel. It was fun, it was messy, and it was heaven. He jumped up and down in the middle of the pan like he was on a trampoline. I could not refill the pan fast enough for him. He splashed in and out, in and out, in and out, leaving a trail of tiny footprints everywhere.

Pooh made mud pies, floated and then tried to drown a plastic ball. He washed acorns, twigs, and even a beetle that happened to be in the wrong place at the wrong time. When he dragged over one of my tennis shoes to give it a bath, I decided that was enough water sport for one day. Besides, I was getting drenched.

Once back in the house, he discovered the dog water bowl and the bowl of dog kibble next to it. I could just imagine hearing him tell himself, "I know what this is!" Fifteen minutes later, the kibble bowl was empty, and the water bowl looked like beef stew that had gone bad. I got into the habit of checking the dog water bowl several times a day. I was never disappointed. There was always at least one present in there for Mom to go fishing for. Some of the treasures were unidentifiable after the little gremlin had washed them for me.

Pooh's first ice cube was given to him as a last-ditch effort to keep him harmlessly occupied one day, when I'd had it with everything. The cold feel of it shocked him at first. Soon, he looked like a hockey player banking a puck off everything in sight. The ice cube got smaller and smaller and was finally just a puddle. Pooh felt all around, looked behind and under everything, and began to get very agitated. I could always tell when this was happening because he chittered to himself. He looked and looked but he just couldn't find his latest treasure. We had been out on the porch, and he sounded so upset. I went into the house to give him another ice cube. Did he have me well trained or what? He paid close attention while I opened the freezer and pulled out the ice cube tray. From that moment on, whenever he heard me rattling in the freezer, he would immediately stop what he was doing and hotfoot it to the refrigerator. He always conned me into giving him at least one ice cube and never tired of them.

What would he do with his first snowfall? I wondered. When baby spied me putting some ice in my drink, I realized I could never leave a full glass within his reach again. I took to using plastic glasses just in case. Heaven help me if I left a full glass of anything unattended on the end table where I usually sat in the living room. I learned to move with lightning speed when this character was around. Pooh would instantly be on that table with his paws up to his armpits in my drink. He was going to catch that elusive ice…while the glass slowly tipped farther and farther over. I had created a monster.

If it was chilly or raining when I would go outside, Pooh would ride inside my jacket front and occasionally work his way down into the sleeve. As he got bigger, he began to get stuck there. I'd try to pull my coat off without him falling or getting smashed and dealing with him being testy all the while. He did not like being in the rain, and he would climb up my leg as soon as his footpad touched the ground. Maybe he was having flashbacks to the weekend I found him. He could play all day in his cake pan and get absolutely drenched, but if one drop of rain touched him, goodbye!

I tried to keep the fact that I was fostering a raccoon from getting around, but it did anyway. I thought it was me who became very popular with the neighborhood children that summer, though now, I must honestly say Pooh Bear did. The kids did yard chores just for a chance to spend some time with him. It kept Pooh occupied, and I got a chance to do my own work. Pooh learned which children were too loud or too rough and just plain avoided them. I wonder how many other lives were forever touched by his innocent-looking face. How many of those kids still think about the summer that they got to play with Mrs. Bode's raccoons? Looking back, allowing those kids to interact with my raccoons was not a good idea!

Checking Out Time

New humans had to be explored, starting at the bottom and working one's way up.

Pockets were favorite places to pause and explore. "What's it got in its pocket?" Pooh seemed to say. I kept treats in mine for him, but unlucky visitors unwillingly gave up keys, tissues, coins, and assorted other goodies. Putting things back in pretty good shape was not in the raccoon handbook of good manners. He'd usually hand over his stolen loot if you had something good to trade for it. Grapes usually worked if he was hungry enough, but he had to think about it for a while. Returning Pooh admirers would score lots of points if they brought him something shiny that he could have. Plain old snacks were also appreciated. I had trouble keeping a straight face while having a serious conversation with a human that Pooh Bear was checking out.

Everyone who had the honor of meeting this friendly fur ball would eventually ask if they could pick him up. As we talked, the rascal would be diverting their attention constantly. Besides pockets, people's belts, jewelry, and buttons came next on Pooh's list of things to be felt, fondled, tasted, and removed, if possible, for closer inspection. Everyone got frisked and had to take inventory before they departed. Besides, it was kind of hard to start a car without keys that had grown legs and wandered off into the grass somewhere.

Sometimes the shakedown got a little too personal, like when he reached down a man's pants or inside a lady's blouse. I was embarrassed, but he wanted to know what was in there. Perhaps I should have given him some anatomy and biology lessons, or maybe he could just read the books himself. Ears, noses, and mouths were gently explored, too, and Pooh never hurt or scratched anyone during any of his investigations.

Once, he ate my favorite earring right off my ear. It was a good thing it was a small, clip type instead of pierced. I could have watched for it in the litter box, I suppose, but I didn't want it back that badly. Years later, we found part of the earring behind the couch in the extra room.

* * *

One of our neighbors had a picnic one weekend in June, and some of the guests wandered over to see the coon. I warned them that he was unpredictable. Some folks held him anyway, and he actually behaved. One man was especially adamant about playing roughly with Pooh while holding him. This person had on some spiffy new shorts and an expensive shirt. Pooh just had a big lunch. My little bear got overly excited having been handled by so many people, and he wasn't wearing a diaper! Bummer!

Pooh had an obsession about head hair and had to feel mine several times a day at least. Perhaps he wanted to be a hairdresser when he grew up. I would be sitting on the couch watching television in one of my few spare moments and minding my own business. "Vidal Sassoon" coon would get up on the back of the couch and run by me as fast as he could. He would grab my hair in his mouth or paws on his way by and yank it as hard as he could. This, in higher coon circles, is a huge compliment, or so I have been told. One way raccoons communicate is by body language and very rough play. Well, after a few minutes of him galloping by and playfully ripping my hair out, I got a pretty bad headache. But I knew that he must have loved me...a lot!

The only way to get him to stop and calm down when he was like that was to get right in his face and hiss as loud as I could. This shook him up immensely. Pooh would run to the far edge of the couch back, whimper, and wring his paws in hopes of getting my sympathy, and it usually worked. When he pulled stuff like that on my husband, Gordon just said no, and Pooh would simply walk away, glancing over his shoulder and giving Gordon a withering look. Well, whatever works, works.

A Nocturnal Water Sprite

We have an above-ground, twenty-eight-foot-diameter swimming pool, and Pooh was drawn to it from the first time I took him out there. I was still a pretty nervous new mom at that point and didn't leave him loose and alone for one second. What would happen if he fell in the pool and panic set in?

At night and while outside, Pooh was hard to see. Gordon usually sat in the chair on the deck with a flashlight, just in case. I knew Pooh needed to get accustomed to being in the dark and all the noises that go with it, and I love to swim at night. We three had a great time out there. Gordon got home from work shortly after midnight, so Pooh really stayed a night owl. But most of my swimming was done in the afternoons. I would get in the water, and Pooh would watch intently from the wooden deck above. Each day he got more curious and· braver as he saw how much fun I was having in there. Sometimes friends or family would join me, and we would take turns keeping an eye on him as we partied in the water. During this time, coon baby hadn't figured out the pool steps yet, so he pretty much stayed on the deck.

Pooh learned to run along the aluminum railing, staying as close to me as possible while I swam back and forth. Sometimes though, it got to be a little too much back and forth for him. After a while, he would just sit down and scream. If I swam too far from where he was sitting and crying, he would commence sitting up on his back legs, hold his front paws up, and chitter. In raccoon talk, I assumed that to mean, "Come and get me, Mom."

One day, his walkway luck ran out when he was in one of his agitated modes, and he just fell in. I was over to him in a flash even though he was dog paddling quite well, or should I say "coon paddling." As I reached him, Pooh saw me and did the climb-on-to-Mom's-head trick. That felt really good on all the skin not covered by my bathing suit.

Talk about a drowned rat. I sat him sputtering on the deck and he shook himself dry, and all the time he was giving me this dirty look. Pooh's fur dried amazingly fast. This was due to its denseness and some kind of water-repellent coating. So he learned to swim, and I learned to wear a shirt over my bathing suit.

After a few more trial swims with my hands around him, my drowned rat turned into a water fanatic. I would go out the kitchen door and down the sidewalk with him running along behind. As smart as he was, I knew that he knew where we were going. I should have bought him his own suntan lotion and sunglasses. Well, at least I did have a special towel for him.

I could not keep him out of the water, but he never did catch on to just diving from the deck railing. I was not about to demonstrate either with the water being only five feet deep in the middle, so I'd lift him in. Sometimes, between swims, Pooh would run around the pool railing over and over and over. It was just for fun, and then he would head to the deck itself. He still hadn't mastered the steps to the yard and hadn't become bored with being on the deck. He would stop to play with bugs, feel rocks, leaves, twigs, and anything else in his path. And all the while, he was chittering to Mom, keeping me posted on his whereabouts and progress. Wild coon babies and their moms must have a similar communication network. I would "chitter" back, and he would be content with his world.

At night, colored lights shined into the water from the Malibu lamps mounted on every other post cap along the railing. My nocturnal child was quite in awe of them. I often wondered if he could tell the blue ones from the green ones and so on. One night, we went out for our usual midnight swim, and I noticed that one of the lights was not working. I forgot about it and enjoyed the water. Pooh swam over by the malfunctioning light several times and finally climbed the railing to investigate. He looked and looked at it and, of course, chittered to himself and me. He ran to the next light and looked at it. Then Mr. Curious ran back to the first one, becoming more agitated. The never-still paws began to investigate the darkened light. He jiggled it harder and harder. It must have been a loose bulb because it finally made contact and suddenly came on. Pooh's voice went up an octave. He rattled it some more, and it began to go off and on, off and on, off and on, over and over. It must have seemed like Christmas for this little elf. He ran to the next light, jiggled it too, and it stayed lighted. Now, totally confused, Pooh ran over to the next one and the next one. He finally tested all eight lights one by one. He sat and talked about it for a while, looked at them all, and saw that they were all lit. I was laughing my head off by now. I almost fainted when he finally swam over to the light that originally caught his attention. He actually knew which light had been the one that he had so much fun with earlier. He played with it, making it go on and off, on and off, until the bulb became too loose and all attempts to get it to work again failed. Pooh Bear lost interest. But for several nights in a row, he had to check that same light out before totally giving up on it.

We had many happy times in the pool swimming together, my Pooh Bear and I. He really came alive at night, with his shining eyes and little wet, furry spikes sticking up all over his back. He would shake himself dry every few minutes only to change his mind and ask to be lifted back into the water for just one more swim before bed. When I got out, I would chitter to him, and he would follow me reluctantly into the house and hopefully to bed.

By now, he was sleeping in the bathroom. I had turned his cardboard box on its side, put a litter box in there, and added new toys one by one when he'd get bored. Sometimes Gordon or I would come in to use the bathroom during the wee hours of the morning. Pooh would just poke his head out for a minute. After seeing who it was, he would go back to bed. First, he would grumble and give a disgusted look. There was no doubt in my mind that he was telling us to keep it down because some people were trying to sleep in there.

TAIL TWO

Pooh Meets a Buddy

A Rude Awakening

Right before the big Fourth of July weekend, Susie called me with the news that I was going to be a mother again. *This is good*, I thought. By now Pooh Bear had become a spoiled brat and needed an attitude adjustment—badly. I had tried so hard not to pamper him and keep life as normal as possible for both of us. Most "only" children get too much attention. I had raised two daughters only eighteen months apart in age, so why couldn't I handle one little raccoon? How much trouble could two be? Pooh was very much into entertaining me and anyone else whose attention he could attract. He could have kept a burglar occupied and amused until someone hauled the robber away. He probably could have taught the thief a trick or two as well. After a few seconds of checking out a new human, Pooh would look at Mom to see my reaction to the stranger. If Mom accepted them, they must be okay and not a danger to a precocious little Pooh Bear.

How I had wished I had a video camera that summer. (I wouldn't have been surprised to see him turn into Ricky Ricardo and do a rumba or produce a top hat and cane and break into "Let Me Entertain You.") But now, Pooh was going to have to share the limelight with someone new. Could he handle it? Maybe. Many of the rehabbers had lots of raccoons of assorted ages, sizes, and temperaments whom they would be willing to pass on to a qualified person. In some cases, they were up to their hips in coons. But each animal was as special to them as my one was to me. These orphans had been through enough without being separated from brothers and sisters; (litters of three to six coon babies are normal.)

I had decided one more raccoon in my life would be all I could handle, so I had to wait for a lone baby to come along. Most raccoon mothers have been killed by cars. The new coon that Susie had found for me had been raised in an apartment. He was reaching a stage where he was becoming destructive and a lot more to handle than a working couple could manage. I could relate to that. It sounded like he needed Pooh Bear as much as my Bear needed him.

I worried about whether the new kid would get along with everyone here and if I could tell these two apart. In most photos and pictures I had ever seen of raccoons, they all looked alike to me. I must also admit that I wasn't sure I would bond with it as well as I had with the first raccoon. Was I in for a shock but not as great as the one coming for Pooh!

I sat at the picnic table and took spoiled rotten brat in my lap and told him his days of being an only child were over. I also told him he better put on his best manners for his new stepbrother. I don't think he was listening too seriously though. He was too busy putting his fingers in my ears, trying to pull off my glasses and counting the buttons on my blouse. Well, we would soon know as the rude awakening was upon us.

Down my long driveway came a car with a strange, furry face peering out of the front passenger seat window. The people in the car—a very nice young lady and her husband—both had sad faces. They got out of the car with an armful of a nervous raccoon. They walked over to where I was sitting with Pooh at the picnic table. He was so busy checking out the new people that he didn't notice anything amiss. The new kid hadn't been outside much and was looking around at everything suspiciously and of course chittering.

After introductions and the stories about our respective animals, I got a close look at the new kid on the block. How different he looked from my little guy. His fur was browner and not as long, and his mask was longer and when I held him for the first time, I realized he was denser and heavier. We guessed he was at least a couple of weeks older than Pooh. The young couple was misty-eyed as they got ready to leave. I asked, as they got into the car, if their youngster had a name. The man replied, "We just called him our Buddy."

I had to hold Buddy tightly when he realized his mom was leaving him with me. His whistle was so sad, and it was then that I knew I could love another raccoon as much as I did Pooh. After Buddy's first set of foster parents left, I took him in the house because he was restless in my arms. I didn't trust him loose in the yard either.

Pooh had been pretty much ignoring the whole situation outside but he could sense that "something" was up. He trotted happily behind Mom on the way inside, pretending that all was well. A nonchalant raccoon is too close to human acting for me. This pretense of not caring about another coon being around continued inside as Buddy began to explore Pooh's turf.

Looking back on Pooh's first reaction, I wonder if he really didn't know I had another raccoon in my arms. If he even remembered, when was the last time he had seen another one, except in the mirror? I will never know what, if any, game he was playing. Pooh finally noticed this other critter, sniffing and chittering, all furry and on four legs. Is it another dog? It was definitely not a cockatiel or a human. Weird!

Pooh Bear whined and wrung his paws in frustration. Then Buddy walked into the bathroom to check out the sleeping arrangements. This invasion of Pooh's private turf was the last straw. Pooh began what I referred to as his "Humpty Dumpty" act. It consisted of arching his back way up exactly like a cat. Next, he went *uh, uh, uh* as ferociously as possible while jumping sideways. Then he put his back end up in the air, all swishing; chest thrust out; and last but not least, teeth bared. It was quite an impressive act to observe but not enough to impress old Buddy. He ignored this weird-acting coon and continued to explore his new surroundings. He was already acclimated to humans and their assorted stuff, so it didn't take him long to look things over.

All this time, poor Abby dog was looking sick and wondering why her humans couldn't just get another dog like normal people. Toto was in the extra bedroom where she had taken up residence since Pooh took over the bathroom. Within an hour, peace was restored, and the two boys really began to check each other out. I could see a light bulb go on in Pooh's head, as if to say, "So I am a raccoon like this other, not quite as handsome as me fellow here." Lucky for all concerned, his new brother and Pooh eventually acted like real brothers!

I thought giving Pooh a stepbrother was going to solve all my problems (or at least half) but instead, they doubled. I thought that maybe they would keep each other amused. What one didn't think of, the other one did, and their personalities were so similar and different at the same time. I thought Pooh was outgoing, but what Buddy lacked in looks, he made up in character. Yes, he was a character all right.

One good thing about Bud being a little older was evident the first time I fed them together. Pooh was still pretty much on the bottle, though he gobbled grapes, marshmallows, and cookies quite well. Bud was already eating real food. When Pooh saw and smelled the choices, he pushed the bottle aside and ran down my leg. He tried to bully his way to the head of the buffet line, and baby never wanted another bottle again.

Bud had been an only child, too, and neither knew the meaning of the dreaded five letter word: s-h-a-r-e. Luckily, their tastes in grub were as different as their personalities. It was amusing how they came to an understanding over who ate what. Well, this pact did not include grapes or marshmallows. Then, it was every greedy coon for himself. At mealtimes, two to three times a day, the mad dash was on. Two little piggies would go digging through the assorted goodies and not-so-good goodies on the aluminum pie plate. I got in the habit of feeding them in the uncarpeted bathroom so I could hose it and them down when they were finished.

Sometimes the meal would go on for hours. Later, my porkies learned to eat in a reasonable amount of time because I took the food away after a half an hour. Enough is enough! Pooh especially liked to eat ham. He also liked cheese, and Bud preferred fruits and eggs and bread and peanut butter. Fighting over grapes was a favorite sport if there were no marshmallows to divvy up. Too many grapes gave them the golly-wobbles, however. I had to count out two little piles of grapes with equal amounts in each. I swear they checked, perhaps even counted, how many each had. If a treat rolled into no coon land, mom had to become a referee, and neither got anything but hissed at. Eventually, the raccoons got slowly weaned to dry dog or cat food, fruits, and veggies as well as things they would find naturally in the wild. I even had someone donate buckets of crayfish, which are a large part of their wild diet. As the boys were weaned from bottles, they got the formula in a bowl thickened with baby cereal. I also added grapes, cherries, etc. As real food began to be provided, the "mush" began to be trashed time after time. Goodbye, baby food, hello, real "stuff." Also, now having teeth, the kits could chew more of a variety. They ate better than us humans and, yes, we had no extra money after grocery shopping!

Bathroom Bunkmates

When I decided to document my first raccoon summer, I was afraid I wouldn't have enough things to write about. Well, it wasn't a problem once I started writing. So Buddy and Pooh, Laural and Hardy, Frick and Frack, Martin and Lewis. Do you get the picture?

I was usually exhausted by the end of the day not from work but from laughing. I wouldn't exchange that summer's experiences with those two (or any of the other raccoon rehab summers that have followed) for a vacation in California. Who has time anyway?

Bud became more outgoing every day while beautiful Pooh Bear seemed to revert more and more to normal coon ways than to ours. Bud partied days and Pooh attempted to do nights. Actually, Bud tried to burn his candle at both ends. He took only necessary coon naps to keep going between his ventures. Both raccoons hated to be put in the bathroom in the middle of the night so we humans could sleep. It became the dreaded place to avoid at all costs.

Some late nights they had to be hauled in there kicking and screaming. Yet fifteen minutes after the two were put in their box, they would be snoring sometimes with those little paws reaching out in dreamland for some faraway treasure. At first, the bathroom wasn't too boring but it was very hot due to a lack of ventilation. I couldn't leave the door open or put a fan in there for obvious reasons. Leaving the one window open and the screen down didn't help if there was no breeze outside.

The only coolish place in the room was the top of the toilet tank, and Pooh had staked that out as his. We have a video of the two of them duking it out over that prized cool spot, and Pooh always won. We wondered if Buddy just did not want to sleep there that badly or if he just argued to agitate his sibling or if Pooh was just more aggressive and determined to keep his space. Every morning, Pooh was on the toilet tank, and Buddy was in the window or elsewhere.

Our bathroom became the worse for wear, and we have since completely remodeled it. Bud discovered one loose tiny inch-square tile in the middle of our handlaid ceramic floor. He just wouldn't rest until he pulled it out. His cohort helped him loosen and pull up twenty or more tiles over the rest of that summer. The tiles would have been easy to glue back in place if we could have found them.

Then, Pooh discovered a loose edge on a corner of the drywall. Over the next four weeks, a two-foot square piece had been torn away bit by bit. The discovery of the toilet-seat lid and the fact that it could be lifted kept them busy, but they never really played in the toilet bowl water. Perhaps having an old laundry tub outside and the pool was enough, but the toilet handle was another matter. It was shiny, and it moved and made a wondrous noise. The day they got strong enough to actually flush it, I was there. When their breathing got back to normal, this became one more thing on a long list of things to avoid. Once, without thinking, I threw an empty pill bottle in the bathroom wastebasket, and Bud retrieved it. He sat and took the childproof cap off in about a minute and proudly handed it to me. I was just glad the bottle was empty.

* * *

Over our toilet were two wooden cabinets, one above the other. They were about three feet long and one foot tall with sliding fronts and storage areas inside. Bud was the first to discover this up-high, cozy place to sleep, and the boys decided that the top of those cabinets would make perfect "raccoon bunk beds." But to reach these beds, it was necessary to climb up on the toilet, then onto the recessed shelf on the side of the wall. Next, they would climb between the wall and the beds and finally descend onto the lower bunk. It was quite a climb and even trickier to get to the upper bunk.

When they were still small, my kids slept together, usually on the bottom bunk. As they got older and the shelf got a little too crowded, they each had their own bed. They liked to sprawl with both left or right legs dangling off the front and they never did fall off. I, however, continued to have minor heart palpitations.

I took out their old sleeping box so there would be more room for food, water, toys and the litter-box. (I wondered if perhaps I could teach them to use the toilet.) While I was gone one day, they trashed the wastebasket, the toilet paper holder, and other things one would normally expect children to get into. I came home to find that everything that had been on the shelves was now on the floor, and my two demolition experts were in the midst of examining their new things.

As I opened the bathroom door, a nauseating combination of smells hit my nose. I knew instantly that I was in trouble or rather, the boys were. The destructive duo were so busy investigating perfume bottles, my special soaps, ceramic knickknacks, silk flowers once in baskets, and air fresheners that they didn't hear me come in. When they finally saw me standing there, scowling with my hands on my hips, and taking in the view of broken glass and the general mess, they both froze in midfeel.

One right behind the other, they ran up on the higher shelf and rung their paws, whimpering in a way that said they were sorry. They were very good at reading my body language and sensed that they were in very big trouble this time. Well, they could run, but they could not hide. I hauled them out to the garage, the duo protesting wildly all the way. I pulled the big doors down, put a washtub full of water on the cement floor, and slammed the door on my way out.

Bud had red lipstick all over him, and they both smelled unbelievably wonderful! When I calmed down and went out an hour later, they were both perfectly clean and very docile. The tub water, however, was pink. I glared at them and said, "Aren't you a nice clean pair. Now, do you want to come into the house and help me clean up the bathroom?" As I left them, I heard two questioning whistles that seemed to ask, "Mom, are you still mad at us?" I never stayed mad at them long because, after one look at those serious faces, I would burst out laughing. Life is too short to hold a grudge for long, especially against two sweet little raccoons.

Kindergarten Capers

typical day for my exploring duo was full of surprises and adventures. Rainy days really got me down because I couldn't let them play outside or coop them up in the bathroom. I couldn't leave them unsupervised for even a minute in the house either. Bud learned to "play" the piano and even turned the piano light on and off. Pooh usually sat listening very carefully for mistakes but showed no interest in playing. Too bad, too, because I could have taught the duo to play "Heart and Soul" or "Chopsticks" and made a fortune. Buddy didn't like when Gordon or I played the piano and covered his ears in disgust. Pooh Bear just left the room. Critics!

Bud was also more mechanically inclined. Besides turning lamps on and off, he learned to do the same with the small table fan. The blades were plastic and Pooh, much to my horror, liked to put his claws in it and make it go *wak, wak, wak*. One day, Gordon was changing a light bulb, and both coons were watching a little too intently. I asked, "Why did you let them see you do that?" He just shrugged and walked away. Sure enough, they couldn't wait to unscrew the bulb and run off with it. They passed it back and forth like a football. It didn't break, but I had trouble getting them to give up their prize. Marshmallows to the rescue again.

I was constantly spied upon, and mental notes were taken of my every exciting move. Pooh sat with the portable telephone in his paws, and Bud would sprawl himself across the base unit on the table. The right combination of buttons pushed would activate the loud beeper, and they loved it. Another time, I was washing dishes in the kitchen and heard, "I'm sorry, but your call cannot be completed as dialed." I hurried in to see two smug-looking animals trying to get the phone to do it again. Pooh handed the phone to me as if to say, "It's for you, Mom." One day, Buddy was lying across the base of the phone having one of his short dozes when the phone rang. He didn't sleep there again, and this time it was for me.

The television remote control was another source of entertainment. Through trial and error, my tiny versions of Siskel and Ebert turned the TV on and also changed the channels. Surprisingly, they were not into nature shows but were enthralled with cartoons. Kids will be kids!

A Four-Legged Flower Child

One day, Abby was acting sick in the dining room, which was never a good sign. I was having a bad day, anyway. I stomped into the room and looked around. I saw nothing too earth-shattering going on. Bud was recycling the trash in the wastebasket, coon style, so I figured it must be Pooh who was in trouble this time. I was bending over, looking under the dining room table, when something light and soft hit my back. "What is this?" I grumbled and picked up a silk flower that had fallen...but from where? *Plop*. Down came another one. And there, up on my six-foot-tall glass-doll display cabinet sat Pooh. He looked like a chubby little Buddha, sitting smack in the middle of a very expensive basket of silk flowers.

I screamed at him, and Abby began to bark. Pooh threw a few more flowers down on me and leaned over to make sure they made it all the way down to the floor and seemed to say, "Yep, they did. Hey, Mom! Love ya, Babe." At that moment, I lost it—patience, temper, the whole ball of wax. Pooh sensed that I might be upset, but he wasn't stupid enough to come down now. He dumped the rest of the posies over the edge, basket and all, realizing he had nothing to lose.

I yelled at him until I was literally red in the face. Bud was whistling at me to calm down. But he should talk. The contents of the wastebasket were all over the living room. Stomping my foot and hissing finally got Pooh moving in the right direction. He shimmied down the cabinet and the stone dining room wall to the floor. Totally out of control. I looked down at these two and what were they doing? Side by side, they were sitting with their paws over their eyes. I started to smile, and the two little masks appeared from behind trembling hands. They seemed to ask, "Is your hissy fit over with yet?" Then, to my wondering eyes, they both hurried over to pick up the flowers and put them back in the basket. "We'll be good, Mom. See we are cleaning it up." Pooh even tried to arrange them all beautiful again for me, but the arrangement never looked the same. And I just left it that way!

Mutant Ninja Coons

While I took a break from household chores to watch my favorite game show on television, the four-legged fiends would also take a break. I would prop myself up with pillows and stretch out on the couch. Pooh usually curled up in a ball on the cushion where my feet were while Buddy would stretch out between the couch's back and me. I'm not a tiny person, and this didn't leave much room for me. I fell asleep one day when we three were sharing the couch and I woke up to very loud snores coming from the two of them. Both were on their backs with one front paw across their eyes and the other draped across my legs. This was the exact same position I was lying in. What were they dreaming about? Hmmmm...Dare I wonder?

After the short nap, we needed a snack to get some fast-food energy. Then it was time for RCW. Oh, for you amateurs, that's Raccoon Championship Wrestling. This interaction and pretend combat was good practice for these two. They needed to sharpen their raccoon skills in preparation for raccoon society. Get real! They just liked to torment each other—and me—in the process.

Abby would usually run upstairs or beg to go outside before all mayhem broke loose. She wanted no part of it, especially when they practiced the Humpty Dumpty act. Buddy was heavier, but Pooh was craftier. In other words, he cheated. It was quite similar to watching professional wrestling. They did some pretty impressive body slams, illegal choke holds, and some moves I've never seen before. If Pooh was on the losing end of a round, he would resort to hitting below the belt with pokes in the eye and a good tail pulling. Nips on the nose and other tender spots brought screams of rage and would escalate into an all-out war.

If one of them caught the other fast asleep, he saw it as a chance to get even in exactly what was considered justifiable revenge. One day, I caught Pooh squeezing Bud between the porch screen door and the inside door. He actually sat back, against the inner door and got a really smug expression on his face. Meanwhile, Buddy's howls of frustration filled the air between the doors.

Bud got even in many devious ways, many of which I never saw. He was every bit as devious as his foster brother. His favorite mode of revenge occurred during mealtime because he was always first in line when food was involved. Bud loved to grab up all the grapes that were supposed to be *shared*. He would push them all under his body, sitting on them so Pooh couldn't have any.

I also observed him pushing Pooh, who was half asleep, off the lower bunk bed in the bathroom one night. Pooh bounced off the toilet and crashed onto the floor. Bud climbed into the lower shelf bunk and slammed the door. This way, he hoped to avoid any plot of revenge on the part of his sibling. Pooh just climbed back up on the toilet, gave a heavy sigh, and went back to sleep. This was just another routine night at the Bode Zoo.

Bud and Pooh acted so human sometimes that it was pretty scary. It was not the same as observing a household pet as it grows in size and skill. Coons are much more complex in their interactions. I wondered how much of what I was seeing was normal raccoon behavior. How many of their experiences here in my home would have repercussions in the wild? They had no fear of humans or dogs. They certainly wouldn't find any bushes growing marshmallows or ham trees in the wild. I had been assured by other rehabber friends that most raccoons revert back to being wild quite quickly. But how did they know how the coons did if they never saw them again?

One lady told me a raccoon named Meatloaf had such an attachment to his baby bottle that he was still clutching it, empty, when they released him back into the wild. Hearing that story somehow made me feel better and more hopeful that my guys would be fine. At least they were weaned from the bottle. Even our best efforts can backfire, I suppose, and all we can do is our best.

Weaning juvenile raccoons to dry kibble, after they have been spoiled, is very much like trying to get human children to eat their vegetables and other things that are nutritionally balanced. Cat food is as close to a healthy diet for raccoons as possible, and dog kibble is also a pretty good choice as a diet. Some of the brands, however, do not apparently smell or taste all that tempting to raccoons.

The first several days I introduced kibble to my coons, they thought it was just something new to trash all over the place, but it became more palatable as they got hungrier. What do raccoons eat in the wild, especially in the winter? Just about everything, I have been told. Meat is not an important part of their diet unless they are desperate. I have since learned that when the temperature drops below freezing, raccoons semi-hibernate and will go for days or longer without food or water or even stir from a hopefully warm shelter.

Backup feeding is absolutely crucial to human-raised animals, especially those released in the late autumn. One can't just dump them off somewhere and wish them luck. That would be cruel, a total waste of our time and efforts as a rehabber, and just plain dumb. Farmers dislike raccoons because they allegedly kill chickens and raise havoc in the cornfields and fruit orchards. Life is hard for all wildlife.

I have tried giving my coons corn every way possible, and none especially liked it. This could be due, in part, to the other choices of foods available. I tried serving corn on the cob, unshucked, which they methodically shredded, washed, and trashed but did not eat. After making the mess, they looked at me as if to say, "Don't give us that stuff again. It might be healthy for us." So in spite of the corn experiment, we never release raccoons near seriously farmed property.

As rehabbers, we are not allowed to release on state-owned property, so this narrows the choices down by quite a bit. We don't want the animals to be hunted or starved or without natural water sources either, so I spend all my spare time looking for good release sites. Many of my neighbors think I am a little crazy to allow more raccoons to survive anyway. They have to deal with coons getting in their trashcans and living under the decks and in their chimneys. They think less raccoons in this world would be better.

I point out the fact that where they, the humans, now live was all a beautiful wooded area a few years ago, and the animals were there first. Also, for every raccoon I save, at least twenty-five are hit by cars in my area. I have a wild opossum living under my porch, and many gray squirrels live in my trees, not without some problems for all. I do not consider them nuisances and feel honored that they chose to live on my property.

The worst problem in my neighborhood is the many cats that run loose. They harass my three dogs, which are in a fenced yard, and my wildlife, which are in cages. Some of the rehabilitators are beginning to feel that if we can't find good release sites, then we shouldn't save animals at all. It is a moral dilemma for us, and it is getting worse every year. I lose sleep and constantly work on ways to make my community aware of what we do and what we need.

I told you that finding Ricky/Pooh Bear or him finding me changed my life forever!

School Daze

Besides getting craftier and bigger, my learning lads got stronger. Now, they could open drawers, cupboards, and almost any unlocked door. They could also help themselves to anything accidentally left on a table. As a result, lids were unscrewed, cereal boxes were opened (usually from the bottom), and canisters of flour, sugar, or whatever made a great improvised sandpile. They helped me fold laundry by playing tug-of-war with socks and underwear. They brought in assorted treasures from outside, usually hidden in their mouths.

One day, the bathroom linen closet was not secure, and every towel and washcloth as well as other assorted linens stored neatly within were flung out—one by one. When the upper shelf was finally reached, they found the light bulbs and cleaning supplies. That was when I intervened. I could not believe the strength and determination to stay put that these two exhibited. I pulled with all my might to remove the mountain climbers and was exhausted when I finally pried them out of there. I should have taught them how to do laundry.

I had to pay massive attention to what we were doing around these miniature Einsteins because they were keenly interested in learning new things. All was tucked in their little computer brains for later use. (Researchers say that raccoons have the ability to remember something for at least a year. They also state that squirrels have a seven minute memory, and a fish remembers for only ten seconds.)

Raccoons also have the ability to teach a learned skill or trick to another raccoon.

They pass skills down from one generation to the next. Thank goodness they are not related to the elephant, which folklore tells us never forgets. That's a mind-boggler. But you know what? I don't think raccoons ever forget…anything…ever!

As I looked· for a permanent new home for the kids, they continued to trash my house and explore the yard. By now, the house had become rather boring, which was understandable since it had been pretty much coonproofed. They had not discovered the closed door to the second floor though…yet. Every day they found something new to check out with those constantly busy little paws. Their front feet resemble hands but even without a humanlike (opposable) thumb, they are still amazingly flexible.

We rehabbers debate whether coons actually wash their food or merely like the feel of whatever they are holding. Does it feel better in the water, which enhances that feeling? I believe both are true, to a point. I observe mine bringing all sorts of strange things to their private pond, the old silver laundry tub. Things alive, or at least alive when they were discovered, edible or not, if it was interesting or felt nice—into the tub it went. There it received a thorough inspection underwater while being put through the wringer so to speak. If the prize was wonderful enough, sibling rivalry would commence, and anyone within ten feet would get wet.

Some days, I couldn't deal with the foster kids in the house for one minute longer. Unfortunately, these times usually fell when it was raining outside, and they couldn't enjoy the freedom in the yard under the watchful eyes of Mom. They went stir-crazy cooped up inside the house, and I went just plain crazy. The only option was to put them in our huge garage, making sure all the doors were shut tightly. I worried about them breaking things, but more importantly, getting hurt. After a few test trials, I felt secure about letting them explore in there.

It was damp, cool, dim and just the kind of place that a raccoon would consider an amusement park. Each day, they chose a new area to explore. They never went back to the same area twice. There were tools and other things that were shiny and felt neat to touch, but they never got hurt. I had their washtub full of water in there, a litter box, and dry kibble so they were entertained for a few days before the boredom set in again.

One day, I went into the garage on one of my many visits to check up on them, and I couldn't find either one. Usually they would come running to the door as soon as I turned the knob. No one was there to greet me this time. I looked everywhere, chittered for what seemed like forever, and began to worry. What if they had somehow gotten outside and wandered off? I sat on the lower step to the second floor (where Gordon hoped to someday put a photo studio).

After an eternity of quiet, I finally heard scuffling noises coming from above. How did they get upstairs like mice? We store all sorts of junk, some furniture, and a few valuables up there. I mumbled to myself, something I did a lot that summer, as I trudged up the steps to see what the storage area had in store for me. When Gordon got home at midnight, he figured out that our little "rats" had climbed up the open studs and shimmied between the step stringer and the studs to reach the landing behind the door, then they just walked up the stairs. By the time he arrived on the scene, it was very quiet up there. So quiet, in fact, that we couldn't determine where they were.

That was another middle-of-the-night adventure I could have done without. We shined the flashlight around and finally got their attention. Two pair of greenish-gold eyes peered down from plywood stored way up in the rafters. I strongly doubt we woke them up though. Judging from their bright expressions, they were asking if the party was over. By now, we had a ladder staged at the appropriate places they liked to climb up into but didn't want to come down out of.

On this particular night, they were even more determined to stay in their newfound tree house. They were just out of reach, and we could not lure them down even with marshmallows so we left them there all night That was their first night away from "home." They spent a lot of time up there after that. We're still finding the poop to prove that.

I don't know what Pooh Bear used for a litter box, but I have a pretty good idea. Buddy would come to the side door and scratch to come in. He would use the litter box and then scratch to go back outside. If the litter box got too dirty, I would get dirty looks. Then they would deliberately dump the contents on the floor and go in the empty pan, making sure I was looking. They trained me pretty quickly to keep *it* cleaned. What would they do when they got back in the wild?

Oil and Water

Pooh headed straight to the second floor of the garage as soon as we'd let them outside. He spent most of his days there napping. Bud thought this pastime was a waste of good energy and only went up to the rafters when he was feeling especially devilish. In other words, he went up to disrupt coon naps. The ruckus that ensued upon Pooh's being rudely awakened made our neighbors shake their heads in dismay. It sounded like a very loud catfight. Luckily, no one fell during these acrobatics and squabbles, but the rafters shook, and Bud usually came down faster than he went up. Grouchy bears who want to practice hibernating should not be messed with!

So Bud got lonely and looked to foster coon mom for company. He became my buddy in the pool, and he actually learned how to dive. Bud also liked to play with the plastic duck that had chlorine in it much as a predator would. One day, he turned it over and got a good whiff of the chemicals and sneezed for half an hour. He didn't keep his paws off the duck, but he always kept it upright when he mock attacked it after that.

I have heard a lot of horror stories about raccoons attacking various feathered fowl and killing them for the fun of it. I tend to think that they are curious and merely want to play, not intending harm unless they are very hungry and desperate.

Bud loved to play squirt-me-Mom from the pool deck and would run back and forth while I splashed him. We had a large fly-shaped insect squirt gun that I would squirt at him and then set down on the deck. He would run up, pick it up in his front paws, and try to squirt me back. By summer's end, he was strong enough to get me too.

One day I was swimming and Bud walked up on the pool deck, rowdier than usual, and I swam over to pet him. He had a scar across his nose from trying to get out of his cage as a youngster, and I didn't need to find any more injuries on him. His fur looked strange and felt even stranger. Upon closer inspection, I noticed that the slippery, sticky stuff was too dark and smelly to be blood. Whatever it was, Bud didn't like the feel of it either and was attempting to lick it off, choking in the process.

Having really attracted my attention now, I climbed out of the water and looked him over more closely. My inspection determined that he was covered in oil. He had gotten into the used oil Gordon had drained out of the car the day before. Was Bud going to be sick or worse from ingesting all that junk? I called our vet, and he said to use turpentine to remove the oil as quickly as possible, and he also said that raccoons are too smart to eat anything harmful. Tell that to the raccoon!

After following the vet's directions, I was left with another problem. How do I get turpentine off a now-very-hyper raccoon? After soap and water, Buddy never looked cleaner, and neither did I. Pooh actually came out of the rafters to observe his brother's discomfort with glee. He enjoyed every minute of it and stayed well out of my reach just in case I had some soap and water left over. We had always been careful with sweet-tasting antifreeze, but now, needless to say, we never left oil, paint, or anything else potentially harmful anywhere our helpful hardware coons could get into.

After Pooh witnessed what to him seemed like an exciting event, he decided he might miss out on something even more exciting. He stopped his days of being a recluse in the garage and took to lounging over a particularly comfortable huge branch way up in our weeping willow tree. He could see Bud and I doing our thing way down below. He didn't have to get involved if he didn't feel like it unless, of course, it involved food. Remember innocent little Ricky (alias Pooh) and his fear of high trees? Now, juvenile Pooh would only come down to use a litter box or if drops of rain began to touch his face.

My personal convenience was not on his agenda, and several times I was tempted to leave him up there when I went away. Buddy always came right to me when I whistled to him, but Pooh would look down from his lofty perch, seeming to say, "What's in it for me?" Waving a whole slice of ham got his chubby, furry body moving with lightning speed, but it had to be a whole slice. Buddy was content with a hug or a pat on the head, and he would go in quietly most of the time, but he got a ham slice too.

Buddy was a very affectionate animal, and he and Abby, our older dog, had many a merry chase around the yard. However, when the neighbor's lawnmower would start, a strange dog would bark, or some other possibly dangerous thing would happen, Bud would look around with panic in his eyes. His I-want-my-mommy cry sounded pretty pathetic. Once I could trust old Bud to stay in the yard, foster Mom only had to hiss and stamp her foot, and he got the drift of where his boundary lines were.

The boys also had a healthy ounce of respect for Charlie, the Old English sheepdog who was kept on a run just to the west side of our neighbor's fence. On the east side of our two acres was the neighbor with the noisy tractor, a table saw, and other assorted threatening human stuff. Only the raspberry bushes and mulberry tree just the other side of the no-no line caused the greedy duo to cross the border. Carl, the neighbor, allowed them to help themselves. Now, they were really learning to find and eat wild and natural food. Carl's wife didn't make many pies that summer, but the free entertainment from the coons was probably worth it.

I promised all my worried neighbors that I would not permanently release my now infamous houseguests on my property. Plus, it would have been much too dangerous.

There were several new subdivisions behind us that were all wooded area less than ten years ago. Also, now a main highway and toll road were just a few hundred yards west of our property on one side, and there was no natural water source nearby.

Where could I take them? They weren't getting any younger, and I was definitely getting older by the minute. Susie and most of the other rehabbers had their favorite release sites, but these areas were getting very crowded. I began putting out the word regarding my need and practically stopping people on the streets of Rockford and the surrounding Winnebago County area. Releasing wildlife in forest preserves or state parks is illegal. And besides, "public" locations are definitely not a good place to put rehabilitated animals of any kind.

Raccoons, especially, lose their fear of humans and dogs. The mischief they might cause people would probably be outweighed by the harm some humans might cause them. My beautiful Pooh Bear made into a hat or good old Bud as part of a coat was too horrible to think about. I do not believe in hunting unless the animal is to be specifically used for food. People who kill wildlife to feel macho or wear the fur to make them look good should rethink their motives. Fur only looks good on the live animal. *Amen!*

Tree climbing became an Olympic event for these two and was important for their survival back in the wild. It would help them escape from hunters and dogs and of course, find some shelter in a storm. They seemed to prefer finding trees with rough bark, and it helped immensely if the branches didn't have thorns on them.

One day, my now-expert tree climbers raced up two trees right next to each other. When they stopped near the tops to catch their breath, chittering began almost at once. They seemed to be saying to each other, "Hey, you are way over there, and I am way over here." They both climbed their way out on some not so sturdy branches, and I held my breath. (Another rehabber had a coon that had fallen from a tree and died, so my concerns were real.)

Pooh had another of his bright ideas just as the branch he was on began to crack. He backed up slowly to the trunk and down he went. He turned his back feet sideways to act as brakes so that he wouldn't break his neck. I heaved a short-lived sigh of relief as he galloped up the tree where Bud was watching with interest and anticipation. This was not a good place for a wrestling rematch, but that's where it took place anyway. They dangled by one paw while batting at each other. Twigs broke off and fell some twenty feet or so to the ground. They somersaulted over one another. They defied gravity with antics so complex and all-out, their limbs hanging over a rock garden many feet below. It was awesome. Both survived a lot better than I did!

Sparklys, Sparklys, Everywhere

Bud and Pooh had mixed feelings about being cooped up in the bathroom at night when instinct told them to go outside and prowl. As they got too big to sleep on a single bunk bed, one would climb the extra foot or so to the upper shelf to sleep. After several nights of climbing and latching a foot around one cupboard to get to the other, one of them accidentally caught one of the closed sliding doors with a back paw.

These enclosed cabinets were where I stored all my makeup, costume jewelry, perfume, and other assorted human female adornments. All this was valuable stuff to a raccoon. I am sure Buddy thought he had hit upon a gold mine. He could hardly wait to show Pooh Bear this gold mine and share the wealth, so to speak. I don't think either of the kids got much sleep that night, judging by the look of the room when I staggered in very early the next morning. Barefoot and half asleep, I did quite a tap dance as I made my way across the room.

I looked up at Bud as he lay dangling half off his shelf in a peaceful dreamland. He clutched a favorite sparkly in one front paw while the rest of my jewelry lay scattered everywhere, even in the sink. The dreaded bathroom became more of a dread to me than it was to the coons. Each time I would open the door, I held my breath and wondered what I would find or not find next. And sadly, we have only one bathroom to share!

I had long since put away anything valuable, breakable, or of any possible interest to a midnight prowler. And since even the current toilet paper roll had to be kept in the closet, this made for a very boring bathroom. They still managed to find things to do in there, however. One morning, my surprise for the day was hearing water running in the bathroom where everyone else had been accounted for. I opened the door just a crack so no over-anxious kid could zoom by me and lead me in a merry chase (merry for him, at least). As I peeked in, the first thing I saw was the sink to the left of the door. In the sink was Pooh Bear, and he was taking a bath. He had the cold water going full blast, and his chubby body was blocking the drain quite nicely. The bowl was overflowing onto the floor where Buddy was taking a shower and rolling back and forth in the puddle. Pooh had a washcloth, and soap was all over his front paws, but he was really more interested in looking at his hands and face in the mirror. I left one soapy paw print on the corner of the mirror for over twelve years as a reminder of the day when Pooh made himself all sparkly.

Both coons had many a bath in the sink over the next few weeks. Finally, one of them turned on the hot water by mistake. They never again turned on the faucets in that sink, but they still did enjoy looking at themselves and each other in the mirror. Occasionally, one of them would sleep in there on an unusually hot night, but once they learned something was dangerous, they never forgot it.

Just Say Cheese

I think Bud had a watch or an alarm clock in his stomach because he sure knew when it was time to eat. He never missed a meal for a raccoon or a human. This was part of the reason he weighed two pounds more than his less porky brother. Gordon eats at one o'clock in the morning, and I usually began preparing his meal at midnight. One night, I had his tray sitting on the kitchen counter, and I cut a piece of cheesecake, put it on a plate, and placed it on the tray. Bud strolled by, took a sniff, and checked his "watch." He then decided an extra snack wouldn't hurt. If he was quiet and sneaky enough, he might not have to *share* any goodies he found with you-know-who. His nose zeroed in on where the good smell was coming from. Now, all he had to do was find a way to get to it!

One of foster Mom's ladders would be great, but perhaps those nifty drawer handles would work quite nicely, and they did! All this time (about thirty seconds' worth), I was relaxing in the living room, which was a bad move on my part. You'd have thought I had learned my lesson by now. It was a little too quiet even though Pooh was in sight and out of mischief for a change.

Strange noises coming from the kitchen got me up and moving, just in time for me to see Bud reach his goal. He saw me zooming in on him at about the same time and pace that was a little too fast for his taste. Bud began shoveling cheesecake into his mouth with both paws as fast as he could find room in there for more. I grabbed him by the scruff of the neck, much like you would a cat, and he growled at me even though he had a mouthful. He had eaten most of the slice anyway, so I just put him on the kitchen floor, tray and all, and let him finish pigging out.

Suddenly, I felt a tug on my bathrobe hem, and there was Pooh Bear. He was looking up at me with the saddest eyes and seemed to say, "Where is mine?" There was no way I was going to give him part of Bud's. (Only crumbs remained anyway, and Bud was in the process of licking those up as I watched.) There was only one thing to do at this point. I got the last piece of cheesecake out of the refrigerator and gave it to a gleeful Bear. Of course, Bud, having finished his snack, tried to convince his brother to *share*, in spite of the fact he had cheesecake coming out of his ears! It didn't work.

I was laughing by now and prepared to clean up yet another mess. By the time my husband came home, I had everything back to normal, and the boys had cleaned themselves up too. Gordon looked at his dinner tray and saw that there was no cheesecake. He looked in the refrigerator, asking where it was. I began laughing all over again as I told him what happened. The coons both looked at me and then at each other as if to say, "We didn't think it was quite that funny. It was good…but not that funny."

Hide-and-Seek

The bathroom was the raccoons' playground, but how long can a coon be amused in there, especially when he comes to think of it as a jail? There were so many other places in the house that had not yet been explored. Getting them to go back to the bathroom for what remained of the night, while humans slept, became quite a chore. By August, it took both Gordon and me to round them up. Sometimes the chase would take half an hour or more. They looked upon all this as some sort of a game of tag and became better at it as time went by.

Behind the heavy, long sofa was the tactic of a last resort as a hiding place for Buddy, but Pooh opted for going under it. Eventually, with their help, the ticking came loose and Pooh could then get up into the springs. He would latch all four of his paws around the wire springs and hang on for dear life. I would tip the couch, and Gordon would pry one paw loose only to have the bear latch it back when Gordon began to pull up another paw. It was a grand game to Pooh. Being older and just that much bigger, Bud could not get under the couch. The first time he tried to follow his sibling under one, he got his furry butt stuck and was hauled out much too fast for his liking.

Once they were in the bathroom, we were ready for a nap. But not the four-legged children who would chitter and slam into the bathroom door over and over again. Basically, they were having a temper tantrum.

Late one night, I had them tucked in and went into the living room to watch some television with Gordon. I sat down and began to get involved in a movie. I just happened to look toward the dining room and here came the brats. They were sauntering along, side by side, with very human-looking smirks on their faces. Gordon commented that he thought I had sent them to bed. I mumbled that I thought I had, too, and he suggested that perhaps I had not latched the bathroom door all the way.

Round two of the game was about to begin, and I was not smirking. I put them back in their prison, and they were very upset as I made sure the door was tightly closed this time. Before I even made it back to the living room, our escape artists were hot on my heels, quite pleased with themselves. I was not amused.

At 3:00 AM, we each had a very wide-awake coon by the scruff of the neck. We then deposited them on the bathroom floor, and that's where we sat down to watch them. They played in our laps for a while, got bored, and finally climbed down out of our laps and forgot we were in there with them. Pooh climbed up onto the sink, stopping to admire himself in the mirror and then began to jiggle the doorknob. Bud was down on the floor with the claws of his front paws under the bottom of the door. Pooh turned the knob back and forth, and Bud clawed at the door. Bud pulled and Pooh rattled. They were out of there to freedom in less than thirty seconds!

What teamwork! We were impressed, very impressed, until we realized we had to catch them again. At 4:00 AM, Gordon was attaching one end of a looped rope to the outside of the bathroom doorknob and the other end to the basement doorknob. I think Houdini and Merlin Jr. finally gave up on the door around dawn. I am just so glad I didn't need to get into the bathroom in the meantime.

Feelings

I have already mentioned how I learned to talk like a coon mom and could read their tone of voice and body language. I saw their moods, and they saw all of mine. One day, I was crying over an especially sad movie, and my boys sensed something was not quite right with their foster Mom. They both got into my lap for a closer inspection of my face. They chittered and wrung their paws. Bud put his paws up, patted my face, and carefully wiped my tears with his soft, sensitive paws. He then got right in my face and chittered as if to say, "Are you all right?"

If Gordon and I got into a loud argument, the raccoons disappeared instantly but not for long. Usually, they were behind the couch with one peeking out from each end. When there was a quarrel between us, the coons' reactions were questioning looks and whistles. Sometimes they would intervene by climbing onto our laps or putting their paw up on our legs. These antics would distract us, and we would usually forget what we had been fighting about. You can't argue and laugh at the same time.

Since I began making notes to write this book, I have gained a son-in-law, Frank; a step grandson, Joe; a granddaughter, Annie; and a grandson, Tony thanks to my older daughter Jeaneil. Ah, more young minds to teach about our wild friends and nature's important balance. Our granddaughter, Annie, has helped with raccoon babies the last several summers, and I don't know who had more fun, us, or Annie, or the raccoons!

Every spring, I get telephone calls from family and friends inquiring about our health, what's new, and asking if we have any coon babies yet. If it is April, the answer is probably yes. Susie called one day in mid-August to tell us about some wonderful people who were interested in having us release raccoons on their property. The next Sunday, Gordon, Susie, and I made the one-hour trip to Davis, Illinois, to check things out. We found it perfect for our needs. We met a couple about our age who were raising their two granddaughters and also enjoyed the assorted animal life on their property. They were in the process of building a big release cage when we arrived, and I liked them immediately.

Smiling and friendly, they seemed to have a genuine concern for wildlife and giving our four-legged kids a chance to be real raccoons. They also expressed a willingness to put out dried dog kibble every day, rain or shine, which would be time-consuming and expensive. This family had quite a few NO-HUNTING acres and was surrounded by hundreds more. There was a natural creek, lots of trees, and no busy roads nearby. (By the way, do you know why the chicken crossed the road? She did it to show the raccoons that it could be done.)

It seemed the perfect place, but I still had mixed feelings. We came away from there quite excited, and we believed that old Bud and Pooh Bear now had a good place to learn how to fend for themselves with lots of wild coons to help them. Loretta, the wife, assured us that if the coon boys got hungry for human companionship, she and her husband, Phil, would be there for them.

We made plans to bring the "children" out over Labor Day weekend unless the weather turned bad. Only two more weeks until release time, and they were the longest and shortest of my life up until then. My feelings for my boys were so strong that I knew it would be hard to say goodbye. I had known all along that sometime down the road I would have to give them up (heavy sigh)!

Eggomaniacs

Since my husband, Gordon, eats in the middle of the night after work, I try to be up and fix him a nice meal. Some nights, I am just too tired, and he has cereal, soup, or fries some eggs. I was not too surprised to find that the raw eggs in the lower shelf of the refrigerator were disappearing. I kept them in the carton they came in, and one day, as I pulled it out, I noticed it was empty. I bought some more and gave Gordon a lecture about too many eggs in the diet being bad for you. He just gave me that are-you-losing-it-again look and ignored my comment.

I came out of the bathroom one day and glanced down the hall toward the refrigerator just in time to see an amazing sight. Pooh and Bud, as a team, were pulling open the refrigerator door like they really knew what they were doing. The bigger they got, the badder they got. Once the door was opened, Pooh sat with his back leaning against it like a doorstop. He held out one front paw, drooling in anticipation. Buddy was slowly pulling out the carton of raw eggs and carefully sliding it to the floor with both front paws. Greed was written all over his face. He carefully opened the treasure chest and placed an egg in Pooh's outstretched paw. He removed a second egg and gently placed it on the floor. He then proceeded to close the carton and put it in its proper place on the shelf and close the refrigerator door.

They sat gobbling their raw eggs, shells and all, leaving no mess. Almost every day, they had helped themselves to the eggs and never took more than one each. Oh, to have had all that on video.

One day, as I opened the refrigerator, Bud quickly crawled inside. As I reached for him, he locked all four of his paws around the wire shelf where the eggs were kept. I tried to drag him out, but he growled at me and dug in. Bud was heavy and determined to party hardy in there. Nothing I said or did made an impression on him. I gave up, slamming the door of the fridge shut, making sure his tail wasn't in the door.

"Let me know if the refrigerator light really goes off when the door is shut!" I yelled and then went back to washing dishes. I heard scuffling noises and dishes rattling but no sounds of anything breaking or screams of pain coming from the refrigerator. I hoped that he would eventually get bored and cool off in the process.

Pooh began to chitter and wring his front paws. He looked at me as if to say, "You're not going to leave him in there, are you?" Maybe he was afraid he was missing out on something or was simply jealous. After a few minutes, I couldn't stand it anymore. The crashes from inside were getting louder, and the whining on the outside was getting unbearable.

I opened the door, and Buddy sprang out like he was shot from a cannon. He was green, red, and assorted shades of brown, which I took to be lime Jell-O, ketchup, and gravy. He dashed into the dining room, leaving greenish footprints and trailing grapes. Some ham slices fell as he left. That kept Pooh busy for a minute or two while I took inventory of the damage in the refrigerator.

The carnage was remarkably small; nothing was damaged due to the tightly sealed plastic lids. Good old Tupperware; it's coon-proof. I next tried to figure out how to keep them out of the fridge once and for all. Buddy gave me the cold shoulder the rest of the day, and neither was interested in getting in there again, even for their daily eggs. Maybe it just wasn't a challenge anymore.

Bird Brains

The worst thing that happened while Gordon and I were raising these two now-not-so-little devils reminded us that these were wild animals we were dealing with. We had a pet cockatiel bird named "Rascal," who could pry open the door of her cage. She would sit on top of the drape, fly around the living room, and was used to the dogs. She was curious about Pooh when he was still called Ricky and made baby noises. She kept her distance when the boys got older and began to prowl. I had to pry one coon or the other off her cage on several occasions.

Once, Bud pulled his I'm-going-to-lock-my-claws-and-hang-on-for-dear-life-and-you-can't-stop-me trick when I tried to pull him off the cage. The whole thing came crashing down—seed, water, grit, and other stuff flew everywhere. Luckily, the bird was perched on the top of drapes, screeching her head off. The cage had been sitting on two end tables that were stacked on top of each other. It was quite a plunge to the floor. Both coons played in the mess for a while but weren't impressed with the taste of birdseed. (I should have shown them how to use the Dustbuster and let them clean it up.)

As time went on, Bud at least showed more and more interest in Rascal. She seemed safe enough until the day he climbed the drapes after her. She became spooked and flew down on the floor, which was not a very smart move on her part. I hear this bloodcurdling scream and dashed into the living room just in time to see the raccoon pounce on the bird like a cat. Rascal bit Buddy on the nose hard, and he backed off long enough for her to escape to the top of the refrigerator. The coon was disappointed, the bird was on the fridge hyperventilating, and I was on the verge of a nervous breakdown.

Feathers were everywhere except on top of the Bird's head; she was practically bald. She came very close to having her brain scrambled. It took six months for Rascal to look normal and even longer to act normal. She hyperventilated every time a raccoon came into sight. I kept her in the cage for the remaining few days before the boys would be released. They played with her feathers for hours.

Fortunately, Bud was now spending most of his time outside. Of course, he took more interest in the wild birds outside and shredded feathers he found in the yard. I wonder if coons eat birds in the wild. With their fondness for eggs here, I wonder if they raid nests in the trees, eating the eggs and maybe even the hatchlings.

They never managed to kill anything bigger than a beetle here, at least that I was aware of. They mock stalked the dogs, and Abby just ignored them. Our poor, retarded dog, Toto, didn't know what to make of all this and usually ran to some safe spot to lie down. The coons seemed to sense that something was wrong with her and that made her easy prey. The survival of the fittest! I was fit, but would I survive?

The Stowaway

One hot August day that first year, I needed to go to the grocery store (for more eggs). It seemed that when I brought groceries home, most of the food was for the animals.

Pooh was snoozing up in his tree, but I couldn't find Bud. I didn't have a lot of time to look for him and so, for the first time, I went away with them both loose in the yard. As I drove away, I wondered where Buddy was and what he was doing, but I didn't wonder for long. Halfway to the grocery store, I suddenly discovered a very furry passenger, and he wasn't wearing a seat belt!

I wondered, *Do I drive all the way back home and drop Bud off, or do I continue on my way and take my chances?* I would have to leave him in the car while I ran my errands, but there wasn't much in there for him to trash. I decided to go for it. I called Gordon at home to tell him I had Bud with me and that he find his missing brother.

He inspected the gas pedal and the brake pedal and got a firm hiss for his trouble. He finally gave up on trying to cause an accident except for a quick readjustment of the rearview mirror. He changed the stations on the radio, and when he got to a heavy metal song, he turned the volume way up and began to rock and roll. Next, Bud adjusted the air-conditioning, and finally, when the rest of the car proved too boring, he just sat in the passenger seat, arms crossed, looking out the window. I was very surprised that we didn't cause a crash. Quite a few other drivers were giving my van interior second and third looks. Next, Bud discovered the electric switches to make the doors lock and the windows go up and down.

Thankfully, we had finally arrived at the grocery store, and I could shut off the engine. It was going to be a very long ride home, but Buddy would have the groceries to keep him more amused on the way back; my car is a minivan, and there is no trunk. When I came out of the market, there were five or six people standing around my van and watching Bud, who was doing his best to entertain his audience. I explained to the crowd that Buddy was going back to the wild soon, very soon, and I got in the car.

Bud wasn't his usual enthusiastic self on the trip home. In fact, he was acting quite strange, even for him. He kept wringing his front paws, chittering, and acting very restless and uneasy. I was still puzzling over his attitude when I stopped at Susie's house. I didn't stay puzzled for long. I got out of the van, and this very familiar aroma drifted from where I had been sitting. Bud had been alone in the car too long, and there was no litter box he could use. The best he could do was "doo-doo" on my car seat onto the beaded chair cover I sit on when I drive. The doo-doo had worked its way down between the beads where I couldn't see it, and when I sat down, well...*squish*. Needless to say, I didn't stay at Susie's for long and didn't go into her house at all. She thought it was pretty funny, and judging by the look on Bud's face when I got back in the car, so did he.

Bud rode across my shoulders on the way home, and when we got there, I gave him a good whiff of the back of my slacks. He curled up his nose in disgust and ran into the garage. He probably woke his napping brother to tell him all about his big adventure. I wonder what it would have been like if they had both stowed away in the van. I have never spanked or hit either raccoon, but sometimes I sure thought about it. Boy, did I think about! I felt that because they were wild animals living unnatural lifestyles in captivity, their antics were not their fault.

Ups and Downs

J ust weeks to go and the "terrors of the seven seas" seemed to know it. They figured out how to open the doors to the second floor and galloped up there one day just a step ahead of me, as usual. Up they went to mysterious new places to explore. Here were new drawers, closets, and beds. Oh my! Pooh tore all the ticking off the bottom of our double bed box springs and made a comfy nest up in it. Wasn't that special? Even years later, we still haven't gotten around to fixing that ticking. Pooh curled up in his new beddy-bye, and Buddy checked out the rest of the upstairs.

There really wasn't anything up there for them to damage, and it became a good place to ship the boys off when we had company. I would be entertaining guests in the kitchen (at the table), and the door to the upstairs would be closed. It was situated right behind where I sat. Some people didn't know that we were raising two raccoons. I loved to watch the expressions on people's faces when old Bud would gallop up and down the hall and steps. I would continue to talk, and the person would finally ask me if I could hear that noise overhead. It sounded like a bowling ball, and I would smile and inform them that it was just our children playing. Then I would open up the door, and Buddy would come flying into my arms, much to the amazement of my guests. (Don't try this at home.) We then all had a good laugh over it.

Once, Bud wanted to come down when I preferred to have him stay up on the second floor. I propped my chair in front of the closed door. Bud didn't like this much and he told me so. Then, it got quiet...too quiet. I could tell he was right on the other side of the door. I crept over to the door, slowly pulled the chair away, and jerked open the door. I caught him in the middle of tearing up the carpet on the lowest step. Once again, looks said it all: "If you won't let me out, then I will dig my way out." Pooh slept through most of Bud's shining moments, and it's just as well.

We had a college graduation party for our older daughter, Jil, and confined the raccoons to the upstairs because we were using the garage and the bathroom, of course. We wanted everyone to be safe, and with fifty people, we didn't want any mishap. Jil took her turn at going upstairs to check on the raccoons just in time to prevent a tragedy. Having grown since his last visit up there, Pooh had gotten his head caught in the springs of the bed. She pulled him free after a lot of struggling, and he was fine. He didn't go under the bed anymore. He just slept on top.

We'd lock the coons in the garage when we couldn't be with them. Sometimes they forgot where the litter box was or were too busy to bother to use it. Gordon still finds dried, little, brown surprises when he is searching for a mislaid tool.

Because we are not much into traveling, we were rarely gone overnight during that summer. When we were away, Susie usually came over, let out the dogs, and checked up on the raccoons. I would go and visit my parents for a couple of days, and the break was welcomed. (Susie is now back to being a cat person who takes in strays, gets them fixed and healthy, and finds them good homes.)

Most of the new friends I have made since getting involved with Pooh and Buddy have been animal lovers in one way or another. It still amazes me how much finding Ricky (Pooh) has changed my life, for the better, of course.

The "Roofer"

Going out of the kitchen door to the outside became almost impossible if the coons were inside. It was worse at night as they grew older and were drawn to the dark. One night, I was busy keeping Buddy from slipping out on me by pushing him back with my foot. Pooh Bear got by me and out the door, down the steps, and into the yard. Would he just take off never to be seen again or just hang out?

I dove for him, but he went up a tree in the front yard. At first, I thought this was a good thing. I got a lawn chair, sat it under the tree, and waited for him to get bored or hungry. After half an hour or more, he discovered a branch that went over to the roof of the two-story garage. He frolicked across the limb and onto the garage roof, which had four gables. He ran up and down the slopes while I tried to figure out how to get to him. I made sure there were no other ways of escape. He was really trapped on the roof except for that one branch.

Pooh was getting wilder and crazier with every passing moment and was in great danger of falling from two stories. I had to get him off there, and none of our ladders were long enough. I went to the second floor of the garage and listened to him charging up and down the peaks and valleys of the roof. It was deafening. He must have been unleashing all his stored-up energy from all those naps he had taken.

I could hear Bud at the kitchen screen door chittering his head off because for once, he was left out of the fun. The dogs were all barking, even the retarded one, and it was like a three-ring circus. How could I get Pooh off the roof? I doubted he would just go back out over the branch, down the tree, and into my arms, even for a slice of ham.

So I crawled up in the second-floor window, leaned out, and got his attention as he dashed by that particular window. He paused to look down on me and was off again. By now, I knew him too well and was certain he would be back. A couple of minutes went by and, sure enough, here he came. The first trip by the window, he just stuck his head in and went on his merry way. Santa would have been proud of his rooftop agility. Next, Pooh came halfway in the window before he charged off again. Finally, he came all the way inside, and I was right there to slam the window shut. To my surprise, Pooh, exhausted, came right into my arms.

Teenagers from Hell

There comes a time in the life of a restless raccoon, as with all living things, when he or she begins to have raging hormones. We rehabbers refer to this time in a coon's life as being a "Teenager from Hell." They do not come by this title without a good reason. Too young to be released yet too old to be caged, they sort of float in limbo where they have mood swings, and that's putting it mildly. Bud and Pooh just wanted to sleep all day and prowl all night, preferably unchaperoned.

Maybe they yearned for coonie female companionship and would have asked for the keys to the car if they could have. They lost all patience with me and wanted to do what they wanted to do when they wanted to do it. They didn't want hissy-stomp lectures from Mom. They didn't want much of anything really, and nothing pleased them. Irritable and crabby, they squabbled with each other over nothing and became dysfunctional juvenile delinquents. They trashed the food, the water, the litter box, and the toys every five minutes. They did not want to be held or fussed over in any way. They had absolutely no attention span and growled at the dogs and everyone else. Last, but not the least, one day, while grooming themselves, they accidentally discovered they were males. Enough said about that!

Yet, once in a great while, they would join me for supper at the kitchen table, sit on chairs, and act like perfect gentlemen. I would give them samples of what I was eating, and we would enjoy a rare moment sharing what was left of our precious time together. (We have since solved the problem of controlling teenaged racoons by purchasing a twelve-by-six-by-six-foot chain-link cage for outside. It has made raising raccoons a lot easier. I still haven't found an easy way to say goodbye though.)

I would look in the garage window at them before I went to bed every night, and they were usually pacing back and forth, back and forth. They also chittered at the top of their lungs most of the night and sniffed longingly under the big garage doors. They wanted their freedom, they wanted to go out and cruise for chicks, well, not chicks maybe, but definitely for lady raccoons. If I had kept them any longer, I know that they would have begun to hate me. It was time for release.

Graduation Day

The last couple of weeks with our fur faces were pretty uneventful. We borrowed a camcorder from Susie and got great videos of them swimming with me. We had to put Pooh in the water, as he had pretty much lost his love of swimming. They impressed us with their tree-climbing abilities and exploring techniques. We filmed all the best ways they drove each other, and us, nuts.

It was now Labor Day weekend. They had learned to forage for food in the grass, having been pretty much weaned from people food, especially junk food. I felt proud of the way they handled themselves outside. The day we took videos and still photos of the raccoon teenagers was sort of like a graduation day. It was very hard not to treat these two kits as pets and try to remember who they really were. All the mothering and pampering in the world would not keep them totally safe as teenagers or adults. They had been taught to fend for themselves and be confident in who they really were.

In the case of raccoons, it is a terrible clash of instincts to be raised in a tame, human environment. Thought of the cliché "If you love it, set it free" was coming home to roost with me. Had I been a good enough teacher? Would they be okay?

Graduation day for the raccoons was the beginning of severing the ties to Mom and Dad. As my time with them drew to a close, I backed off on the hugging and kissing. We had little interaction with them at all at the end by mutual choice. Bud still came and sat in my lap on occasion when he wanted to, but my beautiful Pooh Bear had gone almost totally wild.

I still get a lump in my throat when I think about him, my first four-legged foster child.

We have a five-by-seven colored photo of Bud and Pooh hanging on our bathroom wall. In it, they are sitting on the top bunk bed back when they were still my little kids. The wallboards and floor tiles have been replaced, erasing all signs that two little raccoons grew up in there. When we remodeled, we added a beautiful mirror with a hand-carved raccoon on the corner of it. Many friends have brought us raccoon statues and pictures to make the bathroom very unique. Some of them do not look much like real raccoons though, and I should know.

Several of the friends and family who had been supportive during our first raccoon summer came to say goodbye to the boys in the days before they were released.

Everyone wished them well, and some got a little misty-eyed wondering how I could give them up so easily. Not having spent every waking hour with the coons like I did, others didn't understand how it took more love to say goodbye then it would have to have kept them in captivity. Real love is always worthwhile but not easy.

The last night they were here, I went out to the garage and sat on a step, and the boys wondered what was wrong with Mom. They were more friendly and docile than they had been in a while. It was almost as if they knew these were our last few hours together. We reminisced about all the great times we had and the wild adventures they had with me and now would have without me. We hugged and kissed one another, and I at least had a good laugh over their being so loving.

I tried to memorize their silly faces, and every little body marking that made them each special and unique. How different they still looked from each other. How one of a kind their personalities were. When I patted them, I could still tell who was who by the fur texture. Pooh was still a roly-poly, not-so-little bear, beautiful of course, and with much softer fur. Buddy, with the scar across his nose, had a scruffier, rough-looking coat, but was still quite a character. My fuzzy, no longer small, foster children.

Since that first spring, Gordon and I have branched out to rehabbing opossums and squirrel babies. Last summer, we raised our first two woodchuck babies. Raccoons still remain our favorite of all the wild children though. We will forever have a special place in our hearts for our wonderful little people.

Was that last day a graduation for me as well? I learned to be a good raccoon mother, following along to protect and guide them every step of the way. We made sure they remained raccoonish in every way possible. I watched them grow from helpless babies through the terrible twos and finally saw them become teenagers from hell. I had my chance, done my best, and now…only time would tell.

The words to an old sixties song were running though my head then that last night:

> Your graduation means goodbye, I'll watch you leave with just a sigh, I'll be sad, I'll be blue. I'll always love you, but your graduation means goodbye.

Labor of Love

The Labor Day we released the raccoon teenagers dawned beautiful and warm. I had half-heartedly prayed for rain. It was important to release our now young men as early in the fall as possible so they could put on a good layer of body fat and thicker fur coat. We weighed them that last morning, and Bud tipped the scales at eighteen pounds while Pooh Bear weighed in at a little over sixteen (even though his longer fur made him appear bigger).

Part of me wanted to get the day over with, and part of me wanted it to last forever, allowing me to savor every moment. We lured our young men into a big carrier with some grapes and marshmallows. (What else?) Now, to get the show on the road. We took a picnic lunch for all the humans to *share* as well as a bunch of goodies to get the coons through the first few days of freedom.

We arrived at about 1:00 PM and planned on eating our lunch at Phil and Loretta's picnic table with their granddaughters, Amber and Tasha. They were very excited about the raccoons' arrival and could hardly wait for us to let them out of the carrier. Neither could the raccoons.

The coons had cried most of the hour drive over to the release site, and it was upsetting dealing with their distressed calls. This was not their normal chitter, but it was much more pathetic. This did not help my mood any and I cried almost as loud as they did? One or both foster sons had gone doo-doo in the carrier in their excitement, and that really added to the palpable fear already in the air. Since they had pooped, and there was no place to get away from it, they were a smelly mess by the time we arrived.

Not exactly an elegant first impression, but the humans didn't seem to care. They noticed, yes, they cared, no. We two planned to make our getaway while the coons were sidetracked exploring their new environment and getting acquainted with the new humans. We set the carrier on the picnic table, and I opened the door with one hand while holding my nose with the other.

I took Pooh out first, and he seemed reluctant to come out to me. I held him for a minute or two, kissed and hugged him, and told him to have a good life. Pooh Bear walked around, sniffed everyone, gave me a long, last look, and ambled over toward the woods. He stood way up on his hind legs, putting one front paw up as if to say goodbye. Just like that, he was gone. None of us humans ever saw him again.

Although many raccoons come to their feeding station, our friends were never sure if one of them was Pooh Bear. Hopefully, he's out there having a great life, finding a mate, and being a grandfather by now. No female raccoon could possibly resist my beautiful Pooh Bear.

Buddy's release went totally different. I lifted him out of the carrier, kissed and hugged him, and told him to have a great life. I put him on the ground where he sniffed and checked out everyone too. So far, so good. We sat down to have our picnic lunch, and I kept one eye on the woods in hopes of a final glimpse of Pooh. Buddy hung around to *share* our lunch with us and make a complete pest of himself just in case the new humans hadn't been told how talented he was.

They were going to get a crash course in coon antics. The teenager from hell was about to perform for us. Bud proceeded to climb a railing up onto the patio roof. He methodically ransacked every hanging plant there, every plant these nice people had. Loretta laughed it off, but I kept wondering what he would do next. What about after we left? He got into the dog kibble and water; had several wrestling matches with their dog, Heidi; and just plain ran amok. Every time he created a new disaster, I apologized, but the human property owners didn't seem fazed. Next, he snoozed on the patio roof.

While Bud napped, we decided it was a good time to make our getaway. But by the time we got to our van, Buddy was wide awake and skipping across the yard to us. Loretta had to hold him because he tried to get into the van with us. As we started to drive away, she put him down, and he ran chattering after us. We had to stop while Loretta caught him and held him tightly.

Buddy wasn't the only one crying by now. I made the mistake of glancing back out the car window as we drove out of the driveway. Bud was squirming to get away from Loretta, and I could hear him protesting at the top of his lungs. I heard him long after he was out of sight and still hear him in my dreams sometimes. Was I seriously thinking about doing this again next year? Was it worth it? You bet! It was a very long and quiet ride home that day.

When I called later in the week to see how the raccoons were doing, I learned from Loretta that Buddy had slept his first early morning hours in his new "home" on the patio roof overhang. When Loretta came out the first day to let the dog out, Bud reached down and grabbed her hair. She was startled but became used to it as the days went on. There was still no sign of Pooh.

Our new friends out in Davis, Illinois, kept me posted on all raccoons released there, but they kept track of Buddy the longest. He had his one-of-a-kind scar across his nose and also his distinct personality so Loretta knew it was him, scratching at her door at seven every evening for a cookie treat.

One night, right on time, he had arrived for his snack, and Loretta wasn't there. Since his stomach always kept time and he never missed a meal, where was his cookie? Finally, patience not being a coonie virtue, he tore the screen on the patio door just enough to get into the house. He had never been in there before, but he knew the direction that the cookie person always came from. Bud headed right for the kitchen not touching anything else. The cookie monster found the cookie jar, which rattled when he lifted the lid off.

Phil was sleeping on the couch but not anymore. He reached the scene of the crime just in time to see Bud replace the lid. Phil received one of those withering looks I knew so well as Bud passed him on the way back out the torn patio screen door. The amazing part is that he took just one cookie, none to *share* with you-know-who.

Thus ends the adventures of Bud and Pooh or at least the part I played in their lives. Quite a few baby raccoons have been born out at my friends' property since the young men were released there. Perhaps our now adult boys' adventures have only just begun. Perhaps they are telling stories to their children about spending their childhood with humans. In a way, I hope they have forgotten all about us, yet, in the back of my mind, I like to think they remember. I know I always will.

Afterthoughts

Now that you have read about my first summer as a foster mother to raccoon orphans, perhaps you are thinking that there is something you would like to do to help. I must warn you that rehabilitating wildlife is very rewarding but time-consuming and expensive. I do not work outside the home, and my husband not only supports my efforts in more ways than one but also has his own permit. These two things make it a lot easier for me to rehab.

If you see a possibly orphaned wild animal, please be sure it is truly in trouble before you intervene. Every year, many critters are accidentally separated from their mothers by concerned humans. Remember, it is against the law to keep a wild animal unless you have a permit. It is better to let it take its chances in the wild than in your cage or your house.

Remember, too, that it is not worth getting bitten or scratched attempting to save any wild creature, and wild animals do not make good pets!

If you find an orphaned animal, where do you get help for it? Where do you go for more information about becoming a rehabilitator? Maybe you live on a property that would be a great place to release animals and give them a second chance. If you would like more information regarding any of those things, please try contacting one of the following: your veterinarian, local conservation officer, Humane Society, animal shelter, or animal control services. They should be able to put you in touch with a local licensed rehabilitator who can help and could possibly take you under his or her wing for training.

I would love to hear from other animal lovers. I sincerely hope you enjoyed my book!

About the Author

Kathryn (Kathy) Wrasse Bode was always an animal lover, and grew up with a variety of pets. She was born in Wisconsin but grew up in Illinois, where her father was a plumber and her mother a homemaker. Kathy has a younger brother, an even younger sister, was raised Catholic, and after High School graduated from Beauty School.

In 1963 Kathy eloped with her long-time sweetheart Gordon Bode. They raised two daughters while living in Cherry Valley, Illinois. They now also have two grandchildren. In 1988, the Bode family grew again when Kathy brought home an orphan raccoon found at her parents' lake home in Wisconsin. It sure changed their lives forever! Kathy and Gordon continued to raise orphaned wildlife (with permits from the Illinois Department of Natural Resources) for over 20 years. Raccoons remained their favorite. When else can you find a cat, dog, and a monkey in the same animal?

Shortly after their fifty year wedding anniversary Kathy became a widow and retired from wildlife rehabilitation. Yes, she sometimes misses it, but her heart is happy when she thinks about all the critters she released back to the wild. Knowing she made a difference, even for the critters that did not survive, someone cared! Since Kathy was a stay-at-home wife, mother, and homemaker, She didn't have a nine-to-five schedule. As time went on, she realized that most other wildlife rehabilitators had very little time to spare. So Kathy became a 24-7, seven-day-a-week telephone hotline for all wildlife calls. She even had one at 2:00 a.m., patched through by 911, from a man who wanted her to get a flock of birds out of his tree, now!

During "baby season" in the spring, it would not be unusual for her to get over thirty telephone calls a day. So Bode and her took many rehab Training classes so they could give better advice on the phone. Since he worked four to midnight, they volunteered for a lot of middle-of-the-night rescues, including birds and other species they did not rehab at their home. Kathy's favorite rescue was of a pelican in the Cherry Valley lake!

Kathy also gave talks at local schools, various groups, like scouts and 4-H, and began to train new raccoon rehabilitors. Educating the public through newspaper—editorials—helping change local ordinances, and writing stories (110+) for a national raccoon newsletter kept her busy during the colder months. Sometimes, they had to keep Kits all winter because they were born too late to be released in the fall. So much for taking a break!

Lastly, she wants to remind you that wildlife rehabilitators are volunteers and deserve respect and help whenever possible. There were lots of ups and downs, good and bad experiences, and yes, having many orphans die in her hands. Looking back she still smiles every time she walks into that bathroom and looks at the empty shelves where two little raccoons learned how to be big, bad, wild raccoons in the fall.

Kathy would love to hear from other animal lovers. Please contact her at:

Kathryn Bode
P.O. Box 505
Cherry Valley, Illinois 61016

9 781645 843566